Prentice

AMERICA
HISTORY OF OUR NATION

Test Prep With
Document-Based
Assessment

PEARSON

Prentice
Hall

Upper Saddle River, New Jersey
Boston, Massachusetts

Reviewers

Thomas E. Gray
DeRuyter Central School
DeRuyter, New York

Catherine Fish Petersen
Social Studies Consultant
New York State Education Department
St. James, New York

ISBN 0-13-251349-8

3 4 5 6 7 8 9 10   09 08

Contents

Using the *Test Prep With Document-Based Assessment* Workbook

The *Test Prep With Document-Based Assessment* workbook for *America: History of Our Nation* allows you to practice the skills that you need to act as a historian. Using a variety of practice materials, you will read, evaluate, analyze, and interpret different kinds of written and visual documents. You will apply critical thinking and other skills to a number of documents and images that relate to major themes in American history.

Kinds of Practice Materials

The workbook contains four kinds of practice materials: skills practice worksheets, multiple-choice questions, constructed-response questions, and document-based questions. These practice materials include written and visual documents and various kinds of questions that may appear in standardized tests on American history. The best way to prepare for such tests is to practice.

Skills Practice Worksheets

The first part of *Test Prep With Document-Based Assessment* contains skills practice worksheets. The worksheets cover social studies skills that you need to analyze written and visual documents.

Practice Test Questions

Next, *Test Prep With Document-Based Assessment* provides practice in the three types of questions that you may see on standardized tests on American history. Each unit of the workbook includes multiple-choice questions, a constructed-response question, and a document-based question focusing on key topics in *America: History of Our Nation.*

Here are some tips to help you approach these kinds of questions:

How to Approach Multiple-Choice Questions

Step 1: Read the question very carefully. Make sure you understand the question.

Step 2: Read all four answer choices. Even if you think you know the correct answer, check your choice. Reread the question and all the answer choices to make sure that you have not missed a key word in the question or answer.

Step 3: If you do not understand the question, read it again. If you still do not understand the question, or if you are unsure of the correct answer, don't give up. Use the process of elimination to find the answer. Begin by rejecting any answer choice that you know is wrong.

Step 4: Look for answer statements that do not relate to the question. To do so, reread the question. (Remember that sometimes an answer choice is true, but it does not relate to the question.)

Step 5: Look for clue words in the answer choices. For example, be careful of an answer that uses words such as *all*, *everyone*, *only*, or *completely*. It can be wrong because it is too broad or too extreme. A correct answer might use words such as *often*, *generally*, or *at times*.

How to Approach Constructed-Response Questions

In this part of *Test Prep With Document-Based Assessment,* you will work with what are called constructed-response questions. The questions are based on one or more written and visual documents. For example, a constructed-response question could be based on a reading or a graph. It could also be based on a graph and a reading, a graph and a map, or two readings.

Step 1: Identify the subject and nature of the document(s) in the question.

Step 2: Read through the three questions that follow the document(s).

Step 3: Highlight, circle, or number the area of the document or image that helps you answer the question. Then answer the questions in the order in which they appear. Remember to refer to the information in the document(s) to answer the first two questions.

Step 4: Don't forget to use the skills you reviewed in the skills practice worksheets to analyze the document(s).

How to Approach Document-Based Questions

Step 1: Read the introduction to the activity. Read the essay question several times to make sure that you fully understand it. Keep it in mind as you study the documents.

Step 2: Read or study each document. First, make sure that you understand what the document says or shows. Then, decide whether the document is a primary or secondary source. How reliable do you think the information is? What is the point of view of the person who created the document?

Step 3: Highlight, circle, or number the area of the document or image that helps you answer the question.

Step 4: Answer the questions that follow the document.

Step 5: After you have read all the documents, read the essay question again. Write down one or two sentences that give your basic answer to the question.

Step 6: Outline your essay. Think about how to use each document to support your idea. You do not need to use every document.

Step 7: Write your essay. Your essay should have three parts: (1) an introduction that states your answer to the question; (2) a body that develops your answer and offers evidence from the documents; and (3) a conclusion that restates your answer. You should include specific historical details. Work to include comments on documents in your essay.

Step 8: Edit your essay. Read the essay, changing it as necessary to make your sentences clear and effective and to correct errors in spelling and punctuation.

Document-Based Scoring Rubric

Score of 5:
- Thoroughly addresses all aspects of the *Task* by accurately analyzing and interpreting at least ____ documents
- Incorporates information from the documents in the body of the essay
- Incorporates relevant outside information
- Richly supports the theme or problem with relevant facts, examples, and details
- Is a well-developed essay, consistently demonstrating a logical and clear plan of organization
- Introduces the theme or problem by establishing a framework that is beyond a simple restatement of the *Task* or *Historical Context* and concludes with a summation of the theme or problem

Score of 4:
- Addresses all aspects of the *Task* by accurately analyzing and interpreting at least ____ documents
- Incorporates information from the documents in the body of the essay
- Incorporates relevant outside information
- Includes relevant facts, examples, and details, but discussion may be more descriptive than analytical
- Is a well-developed essay, demonstrating a logical and clear plan of organization
- Introduces the theme or problem by establishing a framework that is beyond a simple restatement of the *Task* or *Historical Context* and concludes with a summation of the theme or problem

Score of 3:
- Addresses most aspects of the *Task* or addresses all aspects of the *Task* in a limited way, using some of the documents
- Incorporates some information from the documents in the body of the essay
- Incorporates limited or no relevant outside information
- Includes some facts, examples, and details, but discussion is more descriptive than analytical
- Is a satisfactorily developed essay, demonstrating a general plan of organization
- Introduces the theme or problem by repeating the *Task* or *Historical Context* and concludes by simply repeating the theme or problem

Score of 2:
- Attempts to address some aspects of the *Task,* making limited use of the documents
- Presents no relevant outside information
- Includes few facts, examples, and details; discussion restates contents of the documents
- Is a poorly organized essay, lacking focus
- Fails to introduce or summarize the theme or problem

Score of 1:
- Shows limited understanding of the *Task* with vague, unclear references to the documents
- Presents no relevant outside information
- Includes little or no accurate or relevant facts, details, or examples
- Attempts to complete the *Task,* but demonstrates a major weakness in organization
- Fails to introduce or summarize the theme or problem

Score of 0: Fails to address the *Task,* is illegible, or is a blank paper

Skills Practice 1: Using Special-Purpose Maps

Some special-purpose maps show natural features, such as elevation and climate. Other special-purpose maps show features made by people, such as land use, roads, countries, population density, and battles.

This skill will help you answer standardized test questions like the one below the map. Follow the numbered steps to apply the skill. Then, answer the question on the line provided after the last step.

Mexico: Population

Step 1 Read the title and look at the map to get a general idea of what it shows.

Step 2 Read the *key,* or legend, to understand how the map uses symbols, colors, or patterns.

Step 3 Use the *key,* or legend, to interpret the map. Look for places where the symbols in the key appear on the map.

Population Distribution
KEY
• One dot represents 200,000 people
Lambert Azimuthal Equal-Area Projection

Step 4 State your own conclusion about what the map shows.

_____
_____
_____
_____
_____

According to the map, which statement about Mexico is true?

(1) Northern and southern Mexico have mostly desert climates.

(2) There are no cities in northern Mexico.

(3) Central Mexico is the most densely populated region of the country.

(4) Central Mexico has more rivers than southern Mexico has.

_____
_____
_____
_____
_____

Step 5 Read the question, and test each answer choice to see whether it agrees with your conclusion. Then, test it again against the information shown on the map.

Step 6 Choose the best answer to the question. Write the number here.
_____

Name _____ Class _____ Date _____

Skills Practice 2: Analyzing Graphic Data

When you analyze graphic data, you read and interpret the information represented in bar graphs, line graphs, or circle graphs.

This skill will help you answer standardized test questions like the one below the graph. Follow the numbered steps to apply the skill. Then, answer the question on the line provided after the last step.

Step 1 Read the title to see what the graph is about. Read the labels and the legend, if any, for more specific information.

Step 2 Look at the data to see if you can find similarities, differences, increases, or decreases.

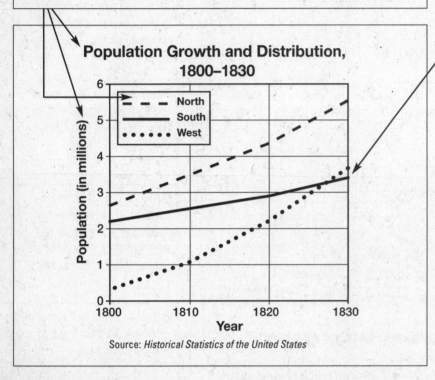

Population Growth and Distribution, 1800–1830

Source: *Historical Statistics of the United States*

Step 3 Make one or more general statements about what the graph shows.

_____
_____
_____
_____
_____
_____
_____
_____
_____
_____
_____
_____
_____
_____
_____
_____

Which generalization about the period from 1800–1830 is supported by the graph?

(1) The West had a larger population than the South did.

(2) The population of the South declined.

(3) The West grew at a faster rate than the North did.

(4) All three regions grew at an equal rate.

Step 4 Read the question, and test each answer choice to see whether it agrees with any of your general statements or conclusions. Then, compare it to the data in the graph.

Step 5 Choose the best answer to the question. Write the number here.

_____

Name _____ Class _____ Date _____

Skills Practice 3: Analyzing Political Cartoons

When you analyze political cartoons, you identify and interpret the symbols, tone, and message. You do the same when
analyzing paintings, drawings, photographs, or posters.

*This skill will help you answer standardized test questions
like the one at the bottom of the page. Follow the numbered
steps to apply the skill. Then, answer the question on the
line provided after the last step.*

Step 1 Read the question, and then study the cartoon carefully. Jot
down what you think is the topic of the cartoon.

_____

Step 2 Identify each
character in the cartoon
by labels and clothing.
Note what each one
is doing.

_____

_____

_____

_____

_____

A GOVERNMENT OF THE PEOPLE
BY THE PEOPLE FOR THE PEOPLE

UNENFRANCHISED

ARE NOT THE WOMEN HALF THE NATION?

Courtesy of the Library of Congress

Step 3 Use your understanding of the figures,
labels, and caption to
draw a conclusion about
the message of the
cartoon.

_____

_____

_____

**This cartoon appeared early in the twentieth
century, before women were *enfranchised* (had
the right to vote). Which of the statements below
best summarizes the view of the cartoonist?**

(1) Women should not get the vote because they are
weak and they depend on men.

(2) Women already have enough power because they
are half the nation.

(3) A nation based on government by the people should
not deny the vote to half those people.

(4) Americans already have justice in the United States
because government is based on the will of the people.

Step 4 Test each answer
choice to see whether it
agrees with your conclu-
sion. Then, test it again
by comparing it to the
cartoon.

Step 5 Choose the best
answer to the question.
Write the number here.

_____

Name _____ Class _____ Date _____

Skills Practice 4: Identifying Main Ideas/Summarizing

When you identify the main idea of a passage, you determine its general idea from its supporting details. When you summarize, you combine a group of main ideas into an overview.

This skill will help you answer standardized test questions like the one near the bottom of the page. Follow the numbered steps to apply the skill. Then, answer the question on the line provided after the last step.

Step 1 Identify the subject.

"Praise to thee, O Nile, that issues forth from the earth and comes to nourish Egypt . . . That waters the meadows, that nourishes all cattle, that gives drinks to desert places . . . Lord of fish, that makes the water fowl go upstream . . . That makes barley and creates wheat, so that he may cause temples to keep festivities . . . He that makes trees according to every wish."

—excerpt from "Hymn of the Nile"

Step 2 Identify details about the subject.

Step 3 Determine what the details tell you about the subject. Write down what stands out as the overall impression.

_____

_____

_____

_____

_____

_____

_____

_____

_____

_____

_____

The passage above is a hymn from ancient Egypt. Which statement best expresses its main idea?

(1) The Nile was important to Egyptian agriculture.

(2) The Nile was a god that demanded praise from his subjects.

(3) The Nile was lord of fish.

(4) The Nile helped ancient Egypt to thrive in many important ways.

Step 5 Choose the best answer to the question. Write the number here.

_____

Step 4 Read the question, and test each answer choice to see whether it agrees with your overall impression. Then, test it again against the details in the passage.

Skills Practice 5: Sequencing

When you sequence, you organize data in order. The data may be organized according to time, importance, or size. Sequencing helps you understand how to get information from graphics such as time lines, pie charts, and flowcharts.

This skill will help you answer standardized test questions like the one near the bottom of the page. Follow the numbered steps to apply the skill. Then, answer the question on the line provided after the last step.

Step 1 Read the title of the time line to determine what it shows.

Step 2 Look at the beginning and end points of the time line to determine its time span. Write down the time intervals into which the time line is divided.

_____

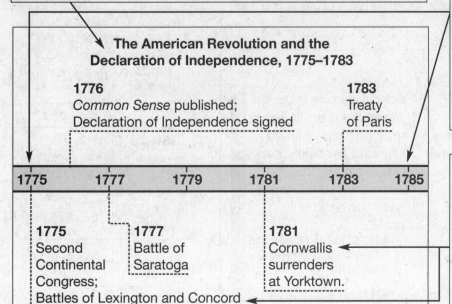

The American Revolution and the Declaration of Independence, 1775–1783

1776
Common Sense published;
Declaration of Independence signed

1783
Treaty
of Paris

1775   1777   1779   1781   1783   1785

1775
Second
Continental
Congress;
Battles of Lexington and Concord

1777
Battle of
Saratoga

1781
Cornwallis
surrenders
at Yorktown.

Step 3 Read all events on the time line. Notice when each event happened. Also, notice how lines connect events and their dates to the time line. Check whether more than one event is included in one entry.

The Declaration of Independence was signed

(1) before the fighting began in the American Revolution.

(2) at the same time the Treaty of Paris was signed.

(3) after Cornwallis surrendered at Yorktown.

(4) after the Battles of Lexington and Concord.

Step 4 Read the question, and test each answer choice. See whether the events in the answer choices are in the same order as on the time line. If not, list the events in their correct time order.

_____

_____

_____

_____

Step 5 Choose the best answer to the question. Write the number here.

_____

_____

_____

Skills Practice 6: Identifying Cause and Effect/Making Predictions

When you identify cause and effect, you understand how an action or several actions led to a particular result. Once you understand the cause-and-effect relationship, you are able to make predictions. *To predict* means to say in advance what is likely to happen.

This skill will help you answer standardized test questions like the one below the book. Follow the numbered steps to apply the skill. Then, answer the question on the line provided after the last step.

Step 1 Read the passage. Then, choose one event or condition as a starting point. Decide whether, in this case, it is a cause or an effect.

_____

Step 2 Look at earlier events or conditions for possible causes. Look for clue words, such as *reason*, *because*, *produced*, *result*, *so*, or *then*.

The Sphinx, an ancient Egyptian monument that was built in Giza more than 4,000 years ago, is now slowly crumbling. One reason is that pollution, wind, and humidity all wear away at the statue. Some attempts at repair have resulted in even further damage. During the 1980s, workers replaced limestone blocks and injected chemicals into the stone, but pieces continued to flake away. Untrained workers have used ineffective repair methods, and vandals have even stolen pieces of the statue.
— adapted from Baerwald and Fraser, *World Geography*, Prentice Hall

Step 3 Summarize the cause-and-effect relationships. Be sure to include all the causes and effects.

_____
_____
_____
_____
_____
_____
_____
_____
_____
_____

According to the passage, the Sphinx is slowly crumbling because

(1) no one is willing to try to save it.

(2) environmental forces are damaging it.

(3) it was poorly built and modern workers are unskilled.

(4) of environmental factors and damage done by people.

Step 4 Read the question, and test each answer choice to see whether it agrees with your cause-and-effect statement. Then, test it again against the facts.

Step 5 Choose the best answer to the question. Write the number here.

_____

Name _____ Class _____ Date _____

Skills Practice 7: Drawing Inferences and Conclusions

When you draw inferences, you determine the necessary results of an assumption. For example, <u>if</u> you assume that *x* is true, <u>then</u> you can infer that *y* must be true. When you draw conclusions, you analyze several inferences to make a reasoned judgment.

This skill will help you answer standardized test questions like the one below the graph. Follow the numbered steps to apply the skill. Then, answer the question on the line provided after the last step.

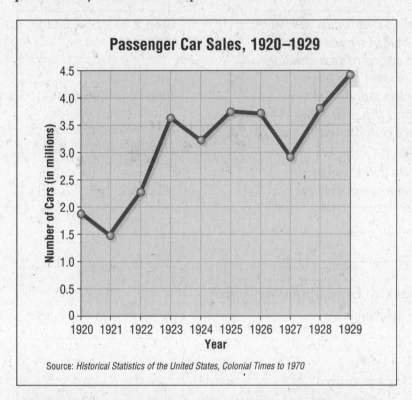

Passenger Car Sales, 1920–1929

Source: *Historical Statistics of the United States, Colonial Times to 1970*

What inference can you draw from the graph?

(1) The <u>U.S. economy</u> was stable during the <u>1920s</u>.

(2) The U.S. economy was unpredictable during the 1920s.

(3) The U.S. economy was expanding during the 1920s.

(4) The U.S. economy was contracting during the 1920s.

Step 1 Determine the topic of the question.

Step 2 Identify what you know to be true. Look at the graph title, labels, and data to determine what they show. Write a summary of what the graph tells you.

_____
_____
_____
_____
_____
_____

Step 3 Determine the connection between the information in the graph and the topic of the question. Use the data in the graph and your knowledge of social studies to make the inference. Write it as an if-then statement.

_____
_____
_____
_____
_____

Step 4 Test each answer choice to see whether it agrees with your conclusion about the information in the graph, your knowledge of social studies, and your if-then statement.

Step 5 Choose the best answer to the question. Write the number here.

_____

Skills Practice 8: Making Valid Generalizations

When you make a generalization, you apply conclusions that you have drawn from a set of facts to a larger situation. To be valid, your generalization must remain accurate for all the examples.

This skill will help you answer standardized test questions like the one below. Follow the numbered steps to apply the skill. Then, answer the question on the line provided after the last step.

"It [the Incan road system] passes over deep valleys and lofty mountains by snowy heights, over falls of water, through living rocks and edges of fast-flowing currents. In all these places, it is level and paved, along mountain slopes well excavated, by the mountains well terraced . . . along the river bank supported by walls, in the snowy heights with steps and resting places."

——*Pedro Cieza de León, sixteenth-century Spanish conquistador*

Step 2 Identify specific facts in the source.

Step 3 State what the facts have in common. Make a generalization, or broad conclusion, about the facts.

_____

_____

_____

_____

_____

_____

_____

_____

_____

_____

_____

Step 1 Identify the subject.

Which phrase best describes the Incan road system?

(1) a marvel of engineering for its time

(2) a steep climb up the mountains

(3) a good route for military invasion

(4) a sign of the decline of the Incan empire

Step 4 Read the question, and test each answer choice to see whether it agrees with your generalization. Then, test it again against the facts.

Step 5 Choose the best answer to the question. Write the number here.

_____

Name _____ Class _____ Date _____

Skills Practice 9: Distinguishing Fact and Opinion

When you distinguish fact and opinion, you separate those statements that can be proved to be true—facts—from those that reflect a personal viewpoint or opinions.

This skill will help you answer standardized test questions like the one near the bottom of the page. Follow the numbered steps to apply the skill. Then, answer the question on the line provided after the last step.

Step 1 Identify facts by asking what can be proved true or false. A fact usually tells *who*, *what*, *where*, or *how much*. Write one fact, and tell how it could be proved true or false.

_____
_____
_____
_____

Step 2 Identify opinions by asking what are personal beliefs or value judgments. Look for words that judge or predict.

Step 3 Decide whether each opinion is supported by facts or good reasons. Write one opinion here, and write facts or reasons that support it.

_____
_____
_____
_____
_____
_____
_____
_____
_____
_____

Geronimo (1829–1909) was an Apache warrior admired for his wisdom. He was also one of the fiercest and most courageous warriors the United States Army ever pursued. When his family was killed by Mexican soldiers, Geronimo vowed vengeance and led his band of warriors in fierce raids. More than once, he was captured, only to escape. In the last campaign, his small, ragged band was pursued by over 5,000 United States troops. Finally, in 1886, Geronimo was forced to surrender.

—*adapted from Davidson and Stoff*
The American Nation, *Prentice Hall*

Which of the following statements from the passage above is an <u>opinion</u>? ◄

(1) Geronimo was admired for his wisdom.

(2) Geronimo vowed vengeance against whites.

(3) More than once, he was captured, only to escape.

(4) He was one of the fiercest and most courageous warriors the United States Army ever pursued.

Step 4 Read the question, and determine what it is asking for. Then, test each answer against your conclusions about facts and opinions. Test it again against the passage.

Step 5 Choose the best answer to the question. Write the number here.

_____

Skills Practice 10: Comparing and Contrasting

When you compare and contrast, you identify how different ideas, objects, historical figures, or situations are alike and/or different.

This skill will help you answer standardized test questions like the one at the bottom of the page. Follow the numbered steps to apply the skill. Then, answer the question on the line provided after the last step.

Articles of Confederation	Constitution of the United States
States have most of the power. The national government is weak.	States have some power, but the national government has the most power.
There is no executive officer to carry out the laws of Congress.	A President heads the executive branch of government.
Only state courts exist. There are no national courts.	Both national and state courts exist.
Congress is responsible to the states.	Congress is responsible to the people.
Congress does not have the power to tax.	Congress has the power to tax.
Each state coins its own money. There is no national currency.	Only the national government has the power to coin money.

Step 2 Identify the main idea of the source you are using. Identify what you know about each characteristic. Write two facts here.

_____
_____
_____
_____

Step. 3 Identify similarities and differences. Draw conclusions, and write them here.

_____
_____
_____
_____
_____

Step 1 Identify the topic and your purpose.

Which of the following statements accurately compares the Articles of Confederation and the Constitution?

(1) Congress had more power under the Articles than under the Constitution.

(2) National courts had more power under the Articles than under the Constitution.

(3) States had more power under the Articles than under the Constitution.

(4) The President had more power under the Articles than under the Constitution.

Step 4 Read the question, and test each answer choice to see whether it agrees with your conclusions. Then, test it again against the facts.

Step 5 Choose the best answer to the question. Write the number here.

_____

Skills Practice 11: Analyzing Primary Sources

When you analyze a primary source, you evaluate a firsthand account of an event for its accuracy, tone, and viewpoint.

This skill will help you answer standardized test questions like the one near the bottom of the page. Follow the numbered steps to apply the skill. Then, answer the question on the line provided after the last step.

> **"The People's Liberation Army (PLA) intervention in Tiananmen was [necessary]. . . . At the beginning, we stressed to our forces, 'When beaten, don't fight back; when scolded, don't reply.' First the PLA fired into the air as a warning. But a small minority shot at the PLA and snatched weapons. Under these circumstances, the PLA had to fire back in self-defense."**

Step 2 Separate facts from opinions. Look for evidence of *bias*, or a one-sided view.

Step 3 Evaluate how reliable the source is. Write your conclusion here.

_____

_____

_____

_____

_____

_____

_____

Step 1 Identify who created the source and when. Determine the main idea of the statement.

_____

_____

_____

This passage is from a 1990 statement released to the press by a Chinese army officer. He had helped direct the army during the mass protest in Beijing's Tiananmen Square in June 1989. There, the Chinese authorities used force to put down the protest. Which statement below best describes how you should use this primary source?

(1) You should not use it because it is from the PLA, which was against democracy.

(2) You should believe it because the officer was on the scene and also had behind-the-scenes knowledge.

(3) You should use it to understand the point of view of the PLA, but be aware that it is probably biased.

(4) You should use only the quote within the passage because a quote must be true.

_____

_____

_____

_____

_____

_____

_____

_____

_____

Step 4 Read the question, and test each answer choice to see whether it agrees with your conclusion. Then, test it again against the source.

Step 5 Choose the best answer to the question. Write the number here.

_____

Skills Practice 12: Identifying Frame of Reference and Point of View

When you identify frame of reference, you understand the influences that shaped the position of the writer or artist. When you identify point of view, you recognize the opinion expressed in a piece of writing or art.

This skill will help you answer standardized test questions like the one near the bottom of the page. Follow the numbered steps to apply the skill. Then, answer the question on the line provided after the last step.

This excerpt from the diary of Mary Chesnut, a southerner living in Charleston, South Carolina, reveals her thoughts as the Confederate army besieged Fort Sumter. The Confederate attack marked the beginning of the Civil War.

. . . *Today things seem to have settled down a little. One can but hope still. [President Abraham] Lincoln . . . has made such silly advances and then far sillier drawings back. . . . Why did that green goose [Major Robert] Anderson go into Fort Sumter? Then everything began to go wrong. . . . If Anderson does not [surrender by] four [o'clock], the orders are he shall be fired upon. I count four, [the church] bells chime out, and I begin to hope. At half past four the heavy booming of cannon. I . . . pray as I never prayed before.*

> —from the diary of Mary Chesnut
> April 8, 1861

Step 1 Determine the topic or issue.

Step 2 Look for direct statements of the person's position and for emotionally charged words. Write down the person's position.

_____

_____

_____

Step 3 Identify what you know about the person's frame of reference, and write down how that may have influenced his or her position on the issue.

_____

_____

_____

Which of the following statements expresses Mary Chesnut's point of view?

(1) She admires President Lincoln and prays that Fort Sumter will fall.

(2) She supports the Southern cause and blames the Union government and army for causing the crisis at Fort Sumter.

(3) She is a pacifist and wants to avoid war at any cost.

(4) She supports the Union, but she is afraid to express her opinion in the South.

Step 4 Read the question, and test each answer choice to see whether it agrees with your statement of the person's position. Test it again against the evidence in the passage. See if it follows logically from the person's frame of reference.

Step 5 Choose the best answer to the question. Write the number here.

_____

Skills Practice 13: Using Secondary Sources

When you make sure that the information you use is reliable, you evaluate the sources you are using for their accuracy, time period, authority, and bias.

This skill will help you answer standardized test questions like the one near the bottom of the page. Follow the numbered steps to apply the skill. Then, answer the question on the line provided after the last step.

Step 1 Identify the date of the source. Determine whether more recent information would be more reliable or whether the information is more reliable because it was written close to the time of the event.

_____

Step 2 Identify the author's qualifications and purpose. Write whether you think the author has a bias.

_____

_____

The following passage describes an 1887 blizzard in Montana. It was written by Teddy Blue Abbot, who was a cowboy during the 1880s. The passage was published in *We Pointed Them North: Recollections of a Cowpuncher*, in 1939.

"The cattle drifted down on all the rivers. . . . On the Missouri we lost I don't know how many that way. They would walk out on the ice and the ones behind would push the front ones in. The cowpunchers worked like slaves to move them back in the hills, but as all the outfits cut their forces down every winter, they were shorthanded. . . . They saved thousands of cattle."

Step 3 Determine how reliable the source is and why. Write your conclusion, and list your reasons.

_____

_____

_____

_____

_____

_____

_____

_____

_____

_____

Which of the following statements is a good evaluation of the reliability of this source?

(1) It is a poor source because it is not current; it was published in 1939.

(2) It is a good source because it is an eyewitness account by a real cowboy.

(3) It is a poor source because the writer does not know how many cattle were lost.

(4) It is a good source because the writer wants you to know what it was like to be a cowboy.

Step 4 Read the question, and test each answer choice to see whether it agrees with your conclusion and reasons. Then, test it again against the passage.

Step 5 Choose the best answer to the question. Write the number here.

_____

Skills Practice 14: Analyzing Diagrams and Charts

Information can be presented as pictures, as numbers, or as text. When you translate the meaning of visual or numerical information into words or you present textual information as a graph, table, or diagram, you are transferring information from one medium to another.

This skill will help you answer standardized test questions like the one near the bottom of the page. Follow the numbered steps to apply the skill. Then, answer the question on the line provided after the last step.

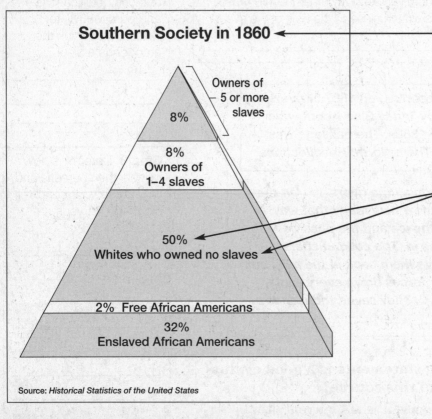

Southern Society in 1860

Owners of 5 or more slaves — 8%

8% Owners of 1–4 slaves

50% Whites who owned no slaves

2% Free African Americans

32% Enslaved African Americans

Source: *Historical Statistics of the United States*

Step 1 Identify the topic of the diagram by reading the title. Then, look at the diagram to get a general idea of its purpose.

Step 2 Identify the key pieces of information. Read labels and numbers carefully.

Step 3 Analyze the meaning of the information. Write down several conclusions that can be drawn from this information.

_____

_____

_____

_____

_____

_____

Which of the statements below best expresses what the diagram shows?

(1) In 1860, most whites in the South owned slaves.

(2) The largest group in southern society in 1860 was enslaved African Americans.

(3) The largest group in southern society in 1860 was whites who owned no slaves.

(4) In the South in 1860, there were fewer whites than African Americans.

Step 4 Read the question, and test each answer choice to see whether it agrees with any of your conclusions. Then, test it again against the information in the diagram.

Step 5 Choose the best answer to the question. Write the number here.

_____

Name _____ Class _____ Date _____

Roots of American History

Part I: Multiple-Choice Questions

Identify the number of the choice that best completes the statement or answers the question.

_____ 1. Which of the following rivers form international boundaries between the United States and its neighbors?
   (1) the Mississippi and the Colorado
   (2) the Ohio and the Missouri
   (3) the Rio Grande and the St. Lawrence
   (4) the Illinois and the Columbia

_____ 2. Which of the following statements BEST describes the way in which archaeologists contribute to historical knowledge?
   (1) They examine court evidence.
   (2) They explain how ancient cultures used objects.
   (3) They put together *archives*, or collections of written works.
   (4) They translate Latin.

_____ 3. Which of the following is an example of the interaction between people and their environment?
   (1) The United States Constitution was written in Philadelphia, Pennsylvania.
   (2) The Pilgrims came to North America from England.
   (3) Native Americans irrigated dry lands.
   (4) Hunters and gatherers moved from place to place to find food.

_____ 4. Which of the following statements reflects the link between geography and population trends in the United States?
   (1) The most recent *census*, or population count, was taken in the year 2000.
   (2) In 2000, about one in every five people was fourteen years old or younger.
   (3) By 2000, the population was about 275 million.
   (4) By 2000, more than half the largest cities were located in the Southwest.

_____ 5. Which belief of Jews and Christians influenced European civilization?
   (1) belief in one God
   (2) belief that the world is made up of atoms
   (3) belief in democracy
   (4) belief in maintaining a balance between people and the forces of nature

_____ 6. Which of these were the two great West African trading kingdoms that arose between 1200 and 1400?
   (1) Zimbabwe and Mali   (3) Songhai and Zimbabwe
   (2) Mali and Swahili   (4) Mali and Songhai

_____ 7. Maintaining a close bond with animals is central to the belief system of which of the following people?

(1) Native Americans   (3) Arabs

(2) Europeans   (4) Chinese

_____ 8. Which idea was developed by the ancient Romans?

(1) direct democracy   (3) republican government

(2) feudalism   (4) the extended family

_____ 9. Which of the following is the prevailing view about how people first reached the Americas?

(1) They crossed a land bridge from Africa.

(2) They traveled by boat from Asia.

(3) They traveled by boat from Europe.

(4) They crossed a land bridge from Asia.

_____ 10. Which of the following is NOT a reason that trade flourished in the Muslim world?

(1) Islam spread rapidly to many parts of the world.

(2) Arabia was at a crossroads linking trade routes from Asia to Africa.

(3) Muslims from all over the world traveled to Mecca to pray.

(4) Muslim armies conquered all of Europe and Asia.

_____ 11. Which of the following is the earliest known civilization in the Americas?

(1) Inca   (3) Aztec

(2) Olmec   (4) Maya

_____ 12. What was the ultimate result of Zheng He's voyages of discovery in the 1400s?

(1) expanding China's overseas trade

(2) spreading the Japanese language

(3) spreading the religion of Islam

(4) expanding trade with Native Americans

_____ 13. Which of the following was a characteristic of life in many African village cultures?

(1) Family relationships were not important to the people.

(2) The people honored the spirits of their ancestors.

(3) The cultures lacked a strong sense of community.

(4) Most people made their living mining gold.

Name _____ Class _____ Date _____

Roots of American History

_____ **14.** Which of the following Native American groups relied on the buffalo to meet their basic needs?

(1) Kwakuitl   (3) Cheyenne

(2) Cree   (4) Miami

_____ **15.** How did the voyages of Christopher Columbus differ from earlier voyages to the Americas?

(1) He was the first explorer to leave a written record of his journey.

(2) He reached Asia by crossing the Atlantic Ocean.

(3) He was the first explorer to sail from Europe to the Americas.

(4) His voyages led to trade between the eastern and western hemispheres.

_____ **16.** Which of the following helped Spanish conquistadors defeat the Aztec empire?

(1) The conquistadors outnumbered the Aztecs.

(2) The Aztecs were weak from fighting among themselves.

(3) A large number of Aztecs died from European diseases.

(4) A large number of Aztecs fled the empire.

_____ **17.** Which of the following statements is TRUE of European life in the 1500s?

(1) Most European rulers permitted freedom of religion.

(2) In England, Separatists dominated other religions.

(3) In France, Catholics and Protestants lived peacefully together.

(4) Most European rulers supported established churches.

_____ **18.** Western European nations sent explorers in search of a northwest passage to find

(1) a shorter route to Canada.

(2) a land route across North America.

(3) a direct route to North America.

(4) a direct water route to Asia.

_____ **19.** What was the purpose of the Mayflower Compact?

(1) to establish laws for the general good

(2) to ensure that only Pilgrims governed

(3) to establish a state religion

(4) to persecute those with certain beliefs

_____ **20.** Which of the following is a reason that the Pilgrims were able to survive early hardships in their settlement?

(1) They built sturdy wooden houses.

(2) Native Americans helped them.

(3) They farmed all year long.

(4) Other colonists sent them supplies.

_____ **21.** Why did the Puritans leave England for Massachusetts?

   (1) to buy cheap land

   (2) to build a society based on biblical teachings

   (3) to start new businesses

   (4) to practice the Roman Catholic religion

_____ **22.** What was the historical significance of the Virginia House of Burgesses?

   (1) It established an official state religion.

   (2) It began a tradition of military rule in the English colonies.

   (3) It began a tradition of representative government in the English colonies.

   (4) It declared Virginia's independence from Great Britain.

_____ **23.** Which of the following was a challenge faced by the Jamestown colonists?

   (1) disputes with the Spanish over gold mines

   (2) the king's refusal to grant a royal charter

   (3) disease spread by mosquitoes

   (4) rivalry with the Dutch over the fur trade

_____ **24.** In which of the following ways did Europe's rulers carry the tensions of the Protestant Reformation from Europe to North America?

   (1) They forced settlers to convert to the new religion of their native country.

   (2) They encouraged settlers to protest their church doctrines.

   (3) They encouraged rivalries between settlers for goods and land.

   (4) They forced settlers to fight one another for the sake of religion.

_____ **25.** What is the primary reason that England passed the Navigation Acts?

   (1) to encourage exploration of the Americas

   (2) to pay for the construction of larger and faster ships

   (3) to encourage trade between its colonies and France

   (4) to tighten its control over colonial trade

Roots of American History

Part II: Constructed-Response Question

DIRECTIONS: *Answer the questions that follow the written document using the space provided. Base your answers to questions 1, 2, and 3 on the reading below and on your knowledge of social studies.*

. . . What then is the American, this new man? He is either a European, or the descendant of a European, hence that strange mixture of blood, which you will find in no other country. . . . Here individuals of all nations are melted into a new race of men, whose labors and posterity will one day cause great changes in the world. Americans are the western pilgrims, who are carrying along with them that great mass of arts, sciences, vigor, and industry which began long since in the east; . . . The American ought therefore to love this country much better than that wherein either he or his forefathers were born. Here the rewards of his industry follow with equal steps in the progress of his labor; his labor is founded on the basis of nature, *self-interest*; can it want a stronger allurement? . . . The American is a new man, who acts upon new principles; he must therefore entertain new ideas, and form new opinions.

—*Michel Guillaume Jean de Crèvecoeur (1735–1813)*

Source: Michel Guillaume Jean de Crèvecoeur, "Letters From an American Farmer,"
An Everyman's Library. New York: J. M. Dent & Sons, Ltd., 1974.

1. What are three characteristics Crèvecoeur sees in the "new" American people?

_____

2. Does this reading give mostly facts or mostly opinions? Explain your answer.

_____

_____

3. How does this reading reflect the growth of nationalist feelings in the new American

nation? _____

_____

Roots of American History

Part III: Document-Based Question

Theme: Origins

This question is based on the accompanying documents (1–8). This question is designed to test your ability to work with historical documents. Some of the documents have been edited for the purposes of the question. As you analyze the documents, take into account the source of each document and any point of view that may be presented in the document.

Historical Context:
In the early years of American history, peoples from many different cultures met and interacted in North America.

Task:
Using information from the documents and your knowledge of social studies, answer the questions that follow each document in Part A. Your answers to the questions will help you write the Part B essay in which you will be asked:

- Describe the relationships among the peoples from many different cultures who interacted in North America from the arrival of the first European explorers and colonists to the mid-1700s.

Part A: Short-Answer Questions
Directions: Analyze the documents, and answer the short-answer questions that follow.

Document 1   Unnamed member of the Ojibwa people, recounting a dream that was dreamt before Europeans arrived (date unknown)

> Men of strange appearance have come across the great water. Their skins are white like snow, and on their faces long hair grows. [They came here] in wonderfully large canoes which have great white wings like those of a giant bird. The men have long and sharp knives, and they have long black tubes which they point at birds and animals. The tubes make a smoke that rises into the air just like the smoke from our pipes. From them come fire and such terrific noise that I was frightened, even in my dream.

1. How did the "men of strange appearance" differ in appearance from the Ojibwa?

_____

_____

2. What are the "long black tubes"? _____

_____

3. Why did the dream frighten the Ojibwa speaker?_____

_____

_____

Document 2 John Smith, describing the "starving time" of Jamestown colony in 1607, from the *General History of Virginia* (1624)

> With this lodging and diet, our extreme [work] in bearing and planting [stockade walls] . . . strained and bruised us, and our continual labor in the [extreme] heat . . . weakened us. . . .
>
> From May to September, [we] . . . lived upon [fish], and sea crabs. Fifty in this time we buried. . . .
>
> But now all our [food was gone], the [fish] gone, all helps abandoned, [and] each hour [we expected] the fury of the [natives]. . . . God, the patron of all good [efforts] . . . so changed the hearts of the [natives] that they brought such plenty of their fruits and provision as no man wanted.

4. Why were the Jamestown colonists in poor physical condition?

_____

_____

5. In John Smith's view, why did Native Americans help the colonists?

_____

_____

6. How did Native Americans help the Jamestown colonists survive?

_____

_____

Document 3 Engraving of Dutch New Amsterdam (from 1651)

Collection of The New-York Historical Society

7. How did the Native American and Dutch boats differ?

_____

_____

8. How did Native Americans interact with the Dutch?

_____

_____

9. What did the Dutch have that the Native Americans might have wanted?

_____

_____

Document 4 Historian John Hope Franklin, discussing the origins of North American slavery, in *From Slavery to Freedom* (1980)

> During its first half-century of existence Virginia had many Negro inden-tured servants; and the records reveal an increasing number of free Negroes.
>
> As time went on Virginia steadily fell behind in [meeting] the labor needs of the colony with Indians and indentured servants. It was then that the colonists began to give serious thought to the "perpetual servitude" of Negroes. Virginians began to see what . . . the Caribbean had already [seen], that is, that Negroes could not easily escape without being identi-fied; that they could be disciplined, even punished, [without regrets] since they were not Christians; and that the supply [seemed to be without end]. Black labor was precisely what Virginia needed in order to speed up the clearing of the forests and the [growing] of larger and better tobacco crops.

10. In the Virginia colony, what two groups does Franklin see as providing badly needed

labor?_____

_____

11. According to Franklin, why did African slavery take root in the Caribbean?

_____

_____

12. What problem led the Virginia colonists to enslave Africans?

_____

_____

Document 5 Historian Louis B. Wright, writing about religion in the colonies, in *The Cultural Life of the American Colonies* (1962)

> The privilege of setting up one's own kind of religion in the new country . . . made a strong appeal to devoted groups. Let no one [think] . . . that [colonists] came in search of "religious toleration." Toleration was [an idea] that few of them recognized or approved. What they wanted was

Roots of American History

freedom from interference by opposing religious [groups] or unfriendly [government officials]. Once firmly in the saddle themselves, [groups] that had been persecuted in England became equally [committed] to [removing those who followed a different religion] from their [colony].

13. What did the colonists mean by *religious freedom*? _____

_____

_____

14. How did the idea of religious freedom attract diverse people to the colonies?

_____

_____

15. How does religious freedom, which the colonists wanted, differ from religious

toleration? _____

_____

Document 6 Gottlieb Mittelberger, writing about German immigrants who became indentured servants to pay for crossing the Atlantic, in *Journey to Pennsylvania* (1750s)

> When the ships have landed at Philadelphia . . . those who [cannot] pay for their passage or . . . give good security . . . must remain on board the ships till they are purchased and are released from the ships by their purchasers. . . .
>
> . . . Every day . . . [people] go on board . . . and select among the healthy persons such as they [think] suitable for their business, and bargain with them how long they will serve for their passage money, which most of them are still in debt for. . . . [A]dult persons bind themselves in writing to serve three, four, five, or six years for the amount due by them.

16. Why did some passengers stay on board ships after they reached Philadelphia?

_____

_____

17. How did people become indentured servants?

_____

_____

Document 7 Olaudah Equiano, an African brought to North America to be a slave, describing the Middle Passage across the Atlantic, in *The Interesting Narrative of the Life of Olaudah Equiano* (1788)

> When I was carried on board, . . . I was now persuaded that I had got into a world of bad spirits, and that they were going to kill me. Their [skin color] too, differing so much from ours, their long hair, and the language they spoke, which was very different from any I had ever heard, united to confirm

me in this belief. . . . When I looked round the ship too, and saw a large fur-
nace of copper boiling, and a multitude of black people of every description
chained together, every one of their [faces] expressing dejection and sorrow,
I no longer doubted of my fate; and [was] quite overpowered with horror
and anguish. . . . I was soon put down under the decks, . . . [but] with the
[horror] of the [smell] and crying together, I became so sick and low that I
was not able to eat. . . . We thought . . . we should be eaten by these ugly
men [but finally] they told us we were not to be eaten, but to work.

18. What was Equiano's greatest fear at the start of the Middle Passage?

_____

19. Why did he feel certain about the fate that awaited him? _____

_____

_____

Document 8   Mercy Otis Warren, describing the growing conflict with Great Britain,
in a letter to Abigail Adams (1774)

I fear . . . that nothing but the blood of the virtuous citizens can repurchase
the rights of nature, unjustly torn from us by the united arms of treachery
and violence. Every [event pushes] this people to look with more impatient
[hopes] for the result of the [Continental Congress]. The [members of
Congress] have an important part to act, a part on which depends in a great
measure the future freedom and happiness of a wide extended empire.

20. Why do Warren and other colonists look to the Continental Congress?

_____

_____

21. Why does Warren fear that blood might be spilled? _____

_____

22. How does Warren reveal her point of view about the conflict between the colonists

and Britain? _____

_____

Part B: Essay
Directions: Write a well-organized essay that includes an introduction, several paragraphs,
and a conclusion. Use evidence from at least four documents in the body of the essay.
Support your response with relevant facts, examples, and details. Include additional outside information.

> • Describe the relationships among the peoples from many different cultures
> who interacted in North America from the arrival of the first European
> explorers and colonists to the mid-1700s.

Name _____ Class _____ Date _____

The Revolutionary Era

Part I: Multiple-Choice Questions

Identify the number of the choice that best completes the statement or answers the question.

_____ **1.** Which statement best describes conditions in North America around 1750?

 (1) The English colonies controlled the East Coast and the Ohio Valley.

 (2) Both the French and the English sought Native American allies.

 (3) France and the Netherlands were claiming English colonies.

 (4) The French were trying to take over farmlands in New England.

_____ **2.** Which of these statements describes a major reason for the conflict between Britain and France in the Ohio Valley?

 (1) French determination to halt westward expansion by the English

 (2) the series of forts the English built along the Ohio River

 (3) the Spanish-French alliance against the English

 (4) French attacks on English colonies along the East Coast

_____ **3.** Which of the following contributed to early British defeats in the French and Indian War?

 (1) British failure to form any alliances with Native Americans

 (2) inexperienced military leadership

 (3) a French alliance with the powerful Iroquois nations

 (4) colonial acceptance of the Albany Plan of Union

_____ **4.** How were British troops able to surprise the French at Quebec?

 (1) by climbing a steep cliff at night

 (2) by rowing into the city's seaport

 (3) by climbing the city walls before dawn

 (4) by storming the city's gates

_____ **5.** What reason did Parliament give for raising taxes in the colonies after 1763?

 (1) Colonists were ignoring the Proclamation Line.

 (2) Colonists did not live in England, but they did enjoy English rights.

 (3) Colonists should help pay for the costs of the French and Indian War.

 (4) Colonists should be punished for protesting against taxes.

_____ **6.** What is one way that Britain punished Massachusetts after the Boston Tea Party?

 (1) Parliament passed the Tea Act of 1773.

 (2) Parliament placed limits on the colonists' right to call town meetings.

 (3) Parliament imposed new taxes on glass, paper, and paint.

 (4) Parliament outlawed the formation of colonial militias.

The Revolutionary Era

_____ **7.** Which new colonial leaders emerged as tensions with Britain grew?
  (1) Samuel Adams, John Adams, George Grenville
  (2) John Adams, Charles Townshend, Patrick Henry
  (3) Samuel Adams, John Adams, Patrick Henry
  (4) John Adams, Charles Townshend, Daniel Boone

_____ **8.** Why did fighting break out at Lexington and Concord in April 1775?
  (1) Minutemen attacked a British fort.
  (2) Colonists refused to let British troops stay in their homes.
  (3) British troops tried to seize colonists' arms and ammunition.
  (4) British troops tried to break up a meeting in the Old North Church.

_____ **9.** What was the historical significance of the Battles of Lexington and Concord?
  (1) The fighting ended colonists' resistance to British authority.
  (2) The outcome proved that militias were no match for British troops.
  (3) Britain gave up any attempt to keep its North American colonies.
  (4) The fighting signaled the start of the American Revolution.

_____ **10.** Which statement BEST describes the mood of the Continental Congress in May 1775?
  (1) Few delegates wanted a formal break with Britain.
  (2) Most delegates wanted to break all ties with Britain.
  (3) A majority of delegates believed that war with Britain was inevitable.
  (4) Most delegates believed that the British king would repeal the Intolerable Acts.

_____ **11.** What advantage helped the Continental army gain control of Boston in 1776?
  (1) greater experience in battle
  (2) use of captured British artillery
  (3) an American naval blockade
  (4) the support of Loyalists in the city

_____ **12.** What action finalized the colonies' independence from Great Britain?
  (1) a mutual agreement with Parliament
  (2) a vote in the Continental Congress
  (3) an order of General George Washington
  (4) a royal decree from King George III

_____ **13.** Which list identifies the three main ideas in the Declaration of Independence?
  (1) natural rights, limits on trade, unjust taxes
  (2) British wrongs, the need for separation, independence
  (3) natural rights, British wrongs, independence
  (4) natural rights, independence, future security

The Revolutionary Era

_____ **14.** How did Britain try to persuade enslaved African Americans to join its army?
   (1) offered them their freedom
   (2) promised they could return to Africa
   (3) offered them large sums of money
   (4) offered to give them Patriot plantations

_____ **15.** What strategy did British commander in chief Clinton hope to use when he shifted the focus of the war to the South?
   (1) to use guerrilla warfare against Patriot armies
   (2) to launch a series of naval battles in southern waters
   (3) to supplement his troops with backcountry southerners
   (4) to use the British generals' firsthand knowledge of southern geography

_____ **16.** Which battle became a turning point of the war because it prompted the French to join the Patriots?
   (1) Saratoga   **(3)** Bunker Hill
   (2) Yorktown   **(4)** Trenton

_____ **17.** Which of these people helped the Patriot cause by seizing British forts on the southwestern frontier?
   (1) Prince Estabrook   **(3)** George Rogers Clark
   (2) The Marquis de Lafayette **(4)** The governor of Spanish Louisiana

_____ **18.** What crucial mistake did British general Cornwallis make that led to the defeat of the British army?
   (1) He attacked Charlottesville.
   (2) He refused to attack Lafayette's troops in the South.
   (3) He depended on Benedict Arnold for reinforcements.
   (4) He disregarded an order and retreated to Yorktown Peninsula.

_____ **19.** Which of the following was NOT one of the terms of the Treaty of Paris?
   (1) Florida was returned to Spain.
   (2) Canada was returned to France.
   (3) The Atlantic Ocean formed the eastern border of the United States.
   (4) Britain recognized the United States as an independent nation.

_____ **20.** Which Enlightenment writer expressed the idea that the relationship between government and the people it governs is a social contract?
   (1) Cincinnatus   **(3)** Cicero
   (2) John Locke   **(4)** Baron de Montesquieu

_____ **21.** Which of the following was a basic idea of the Magna Carta?

    (1) Kings are exempt from the law.

    (2) Most property belongs to the state.

    (3) People have certain guaranteed rights.

    (4) Only kings can declare war.

_____ **22.** Which of the following was a weakness of the Articles of Confederation?

    (1) Congress could not declare war.

    (2) The central government had too much power.

    (3) No court system existed to settle disputes between states.

    (4) Congress lacked the power to coin money.

_____ **23.** To become a state according to the Northwest Ordinance, a territory had to have

    (1) a population of 60,000 free settlers.

    (2) permission from surrounding states.

    (3) a functioning education system.

    (4) a bill of rights.

_____ **24.** Who were two of the leading delegates to the Constitutional Convention?

    (1) Benjamin Franklin and Daniel Shays

    (2) Alexander Hamilton and Patrick Henry

    (3) George Washington and Alexander Hamilton

    (4) Thomas Jefferson and James Madison

_____ **25.** Which of the following was part of the Great Compromise?

    (1) Every state would have equal representation in Congress.

    (2) The Virginia Plan was approved.

    (3) A slave would count as three-fifths of a person in a state's population count.

    (4) Seats in the House of Representatives would be awarded according to population.

_____ **26.** How many states had to ratify the Constitution before it could become law?

    (1) 9 of 13   **(3)** all 13

    (2) 7 of 13   **(4)** 12 of 13

_____ **27.** Which of the following is one reason that states wrote constitutions?

    (1) to give state governments greater power

    (2) to spell out the rights of citizens

    (3) to place limits on individual liberties

    (4) to strengthen their ties to other states

The Revolutionary Era

_____ **28.** Which group argued that a strong national government could be effective and protect states' rights?

    (1) Loyalists   **(3)** Federalists

    (2) Burgesses   **(4)** Antifederalists

_____ **29.** How did the Bill of Rights become part of the Constitution?

    (1) It was agreed upon in the Great Compromise.

    (2) It was agreed upon in the Three-Fifths Compromise.

    (3) It was approved by all the delegates at the Constitutional Convention.

    (4) It was added through the amendment process.

_____ **30.** Patriotism, respect, and responsibility are included among which of the following?

    (1) basic principles of the Constitution

    (2) democratic values

    (3) basic goals of the Preamble

    (4) rights protected by the First Amendment

_____ **31.** Which of the following is NOT a basic goal set forth in the Preamble to the Constitution?

    (1) to form a more perfect union   **(3)** to provide welfare for the poor

    (2) to establish justice   **(4)** to ensure domestic tranquility

_____ **32.** Who are the only elected officials chosen by all American voters?

    (1) senators   **(3)** federal judges

    (2) representatives   **(4)** the President and Vice President

_____ **33.** What is the most important power of Congress?

    (1) fix standard weights and measures   **(3)** make the nation's laws

    (2) establish post offices   **(4)** borrow money

_____ **34.** Which of these lists shows how federal courts are organized from top to bottom?

    (1) court of appeals, Supreme Court, district court

    (2) Supreme Court, court of appeals, district court

    (3) district court, Supreme Court, court of appeals

    (4) district court, court of appeals, Supreme Court

_____ **35.** Which of the following is "the court of last resort," whose decisions are final?

    (1) court of appeals   **(3)** trial court

    (2) district court   **(4)** Supreme Court

The Revolutionary Era

Part II: Constructed-Response Question

DIRECTIONS: *Answer the questions that follow the written document below using the space provided. Base your answers to questions 1, 2, and 3 on the reading and on your knowledge of social studies.*

> . . . A Constitution, to contain an accurate detail of all . . . powers . . . and of all the means by which they may be carried into execution, . . . could scarcely be embraced by the human mind. It would probably never be understood by the public. Its nature, therefore, requires . . . its important objects [to be] designated. . . . That this idea was entertained by the framers of the American Constitution is not only to be inferred from the nature of the instrument, but from the language.
>
> —*Chief Justice John Marshall,* McCulloch *v.* Maryland, *1819*

1. In Chief Justice Marshall's opinion, what does a well-written constitution include? What does it omit? _____

   _____

   _____

   _____

2. What makes Marshall think that the framers of the U.S. Constitution agreed with him on how a constitution should be written? _____

   _____

   _____

   _____

3. Why would Marshall and the framers be concerned about citizens being able to understand the Constitution? _____

   _____

   _____

   _____

The Revolutionary Era

Part III: Document-Based Question

Theme: Rights and Liberties

This question is based on the accompanying documents (1–9). This question is designed to test your ability to work with historical documents. Some of the documents have been edited for the purposes of the question. As you analyze the documents, take into account the source of each document and any point of view that may be presented in the document.

Historical Context:
During and after the American Revolution, the American people held different points of view about the struggle to secure their rights and liberties and to define what they mean.

Task:
Using information from the documents and your knowledge of social studies, answer the questions that follow each document in Part A. Your answers to the questions will help you write the Part B essay in which you will be asked:

> • The history of the United States can be seen as a struggle—not always successful—for rights. How can this theme be seen from the time of the American Revolution to the present?

Part A: Short-Answer Questions
Directions: Analyze the documents, and answer the short-answer questions that follow.

Document 1   Unnamed African Americans, requesting a law to end slavery, in a petition to the Royal Governor of Massachusetts (1774)

> Your petitioners [know] we have in common with all other men a natural right to our freedoms without being deprived of them by our fellow men as we are a freeborn people and have never [given up] this blessing by any . . . agreement whatever. But we were unjustly dragged by the cruel hand of power from our dearest friends and . . . our parents.

1. What is the "blessing" the petitioners refer to? _____

_____

_____

2. What injustices had these African Americans suffered? _____

_____

_____

3. On what ideas did these African Americans base their claim to freedom? _____

_____

_____

The Revolutionary Era

Document 2   Virginia Statute of Religious Liberty (1786)

> Be it enacted by the General Assembly, that no man shall be compelled to frequent or support any religious worship, place or ministry whatsoever, nor shall be enforced, restrained, molested, or burdened in his body or goods, nor shall otherwise suffer on account of his religious opinions or belief. . . . All men shall be free to profess . . . their opinion in matters of religion.

4. What aspect of people's lives did this Virginia law affect? _____

_____

_____

5. How did this Virginia law expand the definition of *freedom*? _____

_____

_____

Document 3   Northwest Ordinance (1787)

> There shall be neither slavery nor involuntary servitude in the said terri-tory. . . . [However,] any person escaping into [the area], from whom labor or service is lawfully claimed in any one of the original states, . . . may be lawfully reclaimed and [taken] to the person claiming his or her labor.

6. How did this law settle the issue of slavery in the Northwest Territory?

_____

_____

7. How did this law affect a slave who had escaped to the Northwest Territory?

_____

_____

8. How did this law both limit slavery and accept slavery as it was? _____

_____

_____

Document 4   Unnamed writer, protesting the fact that New Jersey women who owned property could vote, in a letter to *True American* (1802)

> Timid and [easily influenced], unskilled in politics, unacquainted with all the real merits of the . . . candidates, and almost always placed under the dependence or care of a father, uncle or brother . . . , [women] will of course be directed or persuaded by them.
>
> When our legislature passed the act by which the females are entitled to share in our elections they . . . acted from a principle of justice, [thinking] it right that every free person who pays a tax should have a vote. But from the moment when party spirit began to rear its hideous head the female vote became its passive tool. . . .

⬤

       Female [characteristics] are incompatible with the duties of a free elector.

9. According to the writer, why did lawmakers give women the vote in the first place?

_____

_____

10. Why does the writer think that women should not be allowed to vote?

_____

_____

11. What view of women does this writer present? _____

_____

_____

Document 5   Engraving of African Americans voting for the first time (1867)

12. How does the elderly African American in the engraving show respect for voting?

_____

_____

_____

_____

13. How does the engraving suggest that African Americans had fought for the right to vote?

_____

_____

_____

_____

The Granger Collection, New York

14. How does the engraving reveal its view of voting rights for African Americans?

_____

_____

Document 6   Chinese Exclusion Act (1882)

       The coming of Chinese laborers to this country endangers the good order of certain [areas] within the [country]. . . .

It shall not be lawful for any Chinese laborer to come [to], or . . . to remain within the United States [except those already living here].

No state court or court of the United States shall admit Chinese to citizenship; and all laws in conflict with this act are hereby repealed.

15. What attitude did these lawmakers express toward Chinese workers?

_____

_____

16. What rights did this law take away from the Chinese and Chinese Americans?

_____

_____

Document 7 Photograph of women protesting outside the White House for the right to vote (1917)

17. How does this photograph show the women's determination? _____

_____

_____

18. How were these women trying to get attention for their cause? _____

_____

_____

Document 8 President George Bush, apologizing to Japanese Americans who had been wrongly placed in camps during World War II, in a letter that was sent along with checks to repay them for their losses (1990)

> A monetary sum and words alone cannot restore lost years or erase painful memories; neither can they fully convey our nation's [determination] to [fix] injustice and to uphold the rights of individuals. We can never fully right the wrongs of the past. . . .
>
> In enacting a law calling for [payments for losses] and offering a sincere apology, . . . Americans have . . . renewed their traditional commitment to the ideals of freedom, equality, and justice.

19. How did Japanese Americans suffer as a result of being sent to relocation camps?

_____

_____

20. How does repaying Japanese Americans for their losses recognize their rights?

_____

_____

Document 9 Yuri Sinelnikov, describing why he and his wife left the Soviet Union to come to the United States, in an interview (1970s)

> The first reason why we [left] Russia, it is because we would like to have freedom. . . .
>
> I have freedom here. I can see here not propaganda movies, not propaganda plays, not propaganda literature. I can talk with different people. If I want, I can move [to] another city, [to] another country. Maybe I [won't] go to another country, but I know absolutely exactly that [it] is possible.

21. Why did Sinelnikov and his wife leave the Soviet Union? _____

_____

22. How does Sinelnikov define *freedom*? _____

_____

_____

Part B: Essay

Directions: Write a well-organized essay that includes an introduction, several paragraphs, and a conclusion. Use evidence from at least four documents in the body of the essay. Support your response with relevant facts, examples, and details. Include additional outside information.

> • The history of the United States can be seen as a struggle—not always successful—for rights. How can this theme be seen from the time of the American Revolution to the present?

The Early Republic

Part I: Multiple-Choice Questions

Identify the number of the choice that best completes the statement or answers the question.

_____ **1.** Which of the following precedents did President Washington set at the beginning of his first term?

(1) He decided to move the nation's capital to Washington, D.C.

(2) He established the Supreme Court.

(3) He named well-known, talented leaders to head government departments.

(4) He asked the government to repay federal and state debts.

_____ **2.** Which statement BEST expresses President Washington's beliefs about foreign policy?

(1) The United States should use force when aiding allies in international disputes.

(2) The United States should support permanent alliances with other nations.

(3) The United States should take a more active role in international affairs.

(4) The United States should remain independent from disputes between other nations.

_____ **3.** How was United States neutrality challenged during Washington's presidency?

(1) Britain and France seized cargoes from United States ships.

(2) American merchants continued to trade with Britain and France.

(3) Chief Justice John Jay refused to negotiate a treaty with Britain.

(4) Most Americans wanted to abandon neutrality and declare war on Britain.

_____ **4.** Which of the following resulted from the disagreement between President Adams and Alexander Hamilton about whether the United States should go to war?

(1) The Republican party split.

(2) The Federalist party split.

(3) The Republican party stopped supporting France.

(4) The Federalist party began supporting France.

_____ **5.** How did Alexander Hamilton plan to reduce the national debt?

(1) by requiring states to pay their own Revolutionary War debts

(2) by buying up Revolutionary War bonds and issuing new ones

(3) by refusing to honor debts taken on during the Revolution

(4) by requiring southern states to help northern states repay their Revolutionary War debts

_____ **6.** Which of the following BEST explains why American leaders formed political parties?

(1) to end disagreements over policy

(2) to organize support for their views

(3) to unite farmers and merchants

(4) to follow Washington's advice in his Farewell Address

The Early Republic

_____ 7. Why did the French Revolution lose support in the United States?
(1) The French wanted to stop trading with the United States.
(2) Thomas Jefferson withdrew his support of the French Revolution.
(3) Radicals in France had executed thousands of people in the name of reform.
(4) French reformers wanted protection for the basic rights of citizens.

_____ 8. Which statement BEST summarizes how President John Adams reacted to the crisis with France?
(1) Adams strengthened the navy and asked Congress to declare war.
(2) Adams strengthened the navy but kept the nation out of a war.
(3) To avoid war, Adams gave in to French demands for a bribe.
(4) To avoid war, Adams ignored French attacks on American ships.

_____ 9. Which statement BEST describes a major result of the Whiskey Rebellion?
(1) The new government halted the production of whiskey.
(2) People realized that the new government would execute violent protesters.
(3) The new government proved too weak to respond in times of crisis.
(4) People realized that the new government would not tolerate violent protests.

_____ 10. Which of the following groups decided who won the presidential election of 1800?
(1) the people
(2) the electoral college
(3) the Supreme Court
(4) the House of Representatives

_____ 11. Which statement represents the political views of Thomas Jefferson?
(1) For government to work effectively, the Constitution must be loosely interpreted.
(2) A strong federal government threatens the rights of the states.
(3) The United States should encourage manufacturing and the growth of cities.
(4) The United States should favor ties with Britain over ties with France.

_____ 12. Which of the following is the BEST example of Thomas Jefferson's democratic style?
(1) He ate breakfast at Conrad and McMunn's the morning of his inauguration.
(2) His support of the French Revolution caused some Federalists to worry.
(3) He did not treat the Federalists harshly.
(4) He wore casual clothes and shook hands when greeting people.

_____ 13. From which foreign nation did the United States purchase Louisiana?
(1) Spain
(2) Great Britain
(3) France
(4) Haiti

_____ 14. Why did conflicts between Native Americans and settlers grow after 1800?
(1) Native Americans did not honor treaties with the United States.
(2) Settlers' use of resources threatened the Native Americans' way of life.
(3) Little Turtle tried to drive settlers from the Ohio Valley.
(4) Native Americans demanded tribute from white settlers.

The Early Republic

_____ 15. What formed the route that most western farmers used to ship goods in 1803?
(1) the Appalachian Mountains
(2) the Mississippi River
(3) the Continental Divide
(4) the Atlantic Ocean

_____ 16. Which of the following was NOT an effect of the Lewis and Clark Expedition?
(1) increased knowledge about plant and animal life in the West
(2) immediate settlement of western lands by pioneers
(3) increased knowledge about Native American cultures
(4) a map showing a route to the Pacific Ocean

_____ 17. Lewis and Clark explored a water route to the Pacific Ocean. How would such a route have benefited overseas trade?
(1) It would have increased trade with French and British merchants.
(2) It would have provided a more direct route to markets in China and India.
(3) It would have allowed American ships to evade a blockade of East Coast harbors.
(4) It would have allowed settlers to use the route to find new lands to farm.

_____ 18. Which action BEST reflects Jefferson's determination to reduce the size and power of the federal government?
(1) He kept the Bank of the United States open.
(2) He cut the federal budget.
(3) He continued to pay state debts from federal funds.
(4) He allowed many Federalists to keep their government jobs.

_____ 19. Which of the following was a result of the Embargo Act?
(1) It increased Jefferson's popularity with New England merchants.
(2) It badly hurt American shipping and agricultural activities.
(3) It increased American trade with non-European nations.
(4) It led to Jefferson's defeat in the election of 1808.

_____ 20. Which of the following is a way that BOTH Britain and France disregarded American neutrality?
(1) Both demanded a yearly tribute from the United States.
(2) Both impressed American sailors into the service of their navies.
(3) Both captured American ships bound for Europe.
(4) Both used an embargo to hinder American economic growth.

_____ 21. Which of the following BEST summarizes the goal of Tecumeseh's Indian confederation?
(1) to return to the old ways and to unite the nations to resist white settlers
(2) to get money for Indian lands instead of losing them in battles
(3) to use trade with white settlers to improve the Native Americans' lives
(4) to get all the Native American nations to convert to Christianity

The Early Republic

_____ **22.** Who feared a loss of political influence because of the War of 1812?

    (1) southerners   **(3)** New Englanders

    (2) westerners   **(4)** Native Americans

_____ **23.** Which statement BEST describes conditions in the United States as it entered the War of 1812?

    (1) Canadians were calling for American help to remove British rule.

    (2) The free market had produced a strong economy based on worldwide trade.

    (3) A small army and navy lacked the training to face the British military.

    (4) People from all regions of the country were united in favor of the war.

_____ **24.** Which is the proper sequence of the final events of the War of 1812?

    (1) burning of Washington, D.C.; signing of the Treaty of Ghent; Battle of New Orleans

    (2) Battle of New Orleans; burning of Washington, D.C.; Battle at Fort McHenry

    (3) signing of the Treaty of Ghent; burning of Washington, D.C.; Battle of New Orleans

    (4) Battle at Fort McHenry; Battle of New Orleans; burning of Washington, D.C.

_____ **25.** How did Congress help American industry after the War of 1812?

    (1) It closed the first Bank of the United States.

    (2) It established the second Bank of the United States.

    (3) It encouraged merchants to import British goods.

    (4) It lowered tariffs.

_____ **26.** Congress protected American manufacturers after the War of 1812 by

    (1) banning all imported goods.

    (2) raising tariffs on imported goods.

    (3) lowering tariffs on imported goods.

    (4) eliminating tariffs on imported goods.

_____ **27.** Which of the following is an example of *judicial review*?

    (1) Congress votes to approve a Supreme Court appointment.

    (2) A newspaper editorial criticizes a Supreme Court decision.

    (3) A decision by a lower court is appealed to the Supreme Court.

    (4) The Supreme Court rules that a new law violates the Constitution.

_____ **28.** Which of the following is the BEST interpretation of the Supreme Court decision in *McCullough* v. *Maryland*?

    (1) The federal government cannot tax state institutions.

    (2) States have no power to control federal institutions within their borders.

    (3) States can create federal laws to suit their own needs.

    (4) States can nullify federal laws that they believe are unconstitutional.

Name _____ Class _____ Date _____

The Early Republic

_____ **29.** Which of the following was an unintended result of Henry Clay's American System?
   (1) large amounts of money spent on transportation
   (2) high tariffs
   (3) further growth of sectionalism
   (4) support from southerners

_____ **30.** Which of the following statements describes the Industrial Revolution?
   (1) It was quick and violent and produced few results.
   (2) It took place mostly in rural areas among farmers.
   (3) It depended largely on the development of the factory system.
   (4) It occurred because of years of planning in the United States in the mid-1700s.

_____ **31.** Why was Simón Bolívar known as "the Liberator"?
   (1) He led a revolt that freed Texas from Mexican rule.
   (2) He led successful independence movements in South America.
   (3) His writings inspired Mexicans to seek independence.
   (4) He persuaded Spain to free its Latin American colonies peacefully.

_____ **32.** What is one way in which Americans improved their roads in the early 1800s?
   (1) Congress approved funds for toll roads.
   (2) Private companies put up funds to build the National Road.
   (3) Private companies built turnpikes.
   (4) During the War of 1812, the army built the National Road.

_____ **33.** What is one reason Lowell, Massachusetts, was called a model factory town?
   (1) Factories first appeared in the United States in this city.
   (2) Factories there were the first to employ young children.
   (3) Factory workers there lived in clean, decent housing.
   (4) Factory owners there shortened the employees' workday.

_____ **34.** How did the United States gain Florida from Spain?
   (1) Spain gave Florida to the United States.
   (2) The United States won Florida after a lengthy battle with Spain.
   (3) The United States bought Florida for $5 million.
   (4) Spain gave up Florida as a result of the Monroe Doctrine.

_____ **35.** Which statement BEST describes daily life in a factory in the early 1800s?
   (1) The employees, mostly women and children, worked long hours.
   (2) Factory owners took increasing interest in the welfare of the workers.
   (3) Laws were enacted to prevent child labor.
   (4) The employees, mostly men, worked short hours.

_____ **36.** Which of the following led to the creation of the Monroe Doctrine?
   (1) Americans wanted to claim lands on the Pacific coast of North America.
   (2) Americans wanted to establish control over Latin America.
   (3) Americans feared that Spain would try to regain its colonies in Latin America.
   (4) Americans feared that Britain would try to take over its original colonies in North America.

Name _____ Class _____ Date _____

The Early Republic

Part II: Constructed-Response Question

DIRECTIONS: *Answer each question that follows the written and visual documents using the space provided. Base your answers to questions 1, 2, and 3 on the map and table below and on your knowledge of social studies.*

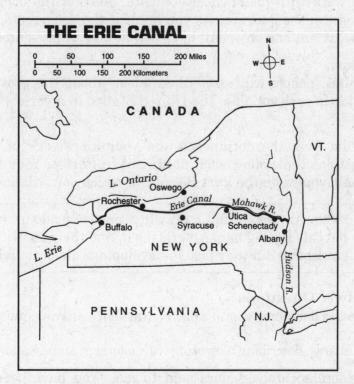

Wheat Cargoes Eastbound on the Canal	
Year	**Number of Bushels**
1829	3,640
1837	500,000
1845	1,330,000

1. What two major bodies of water did the Erie Canal link? _____

   _____

2. In which direction did most freight along the canal travel? Why?

   _____

   _____

3. How did internal improvements such as the building of the Erie Canal affect the

   United States? _____

   _____

The Early Republic

Part III: Document-Based Question

Theme: Nationalism

This question is based on the accompanying documents (1–8). This question is designed to test your ability to work with historical documents. Some of the documents have been edited for the purposes of the question. As you analyze the documents, take into account the source of each document and any point of view that may be presented in the document.

Historical Context:
In the early 1800s, people expressed their ideas about the growing American nationalism (pride in or devotion to the United States) in a variety of ways.

Task:
Using information from the documents and your knowledge of social studies, answer the questions that follow each document in Part A. Your answers to the questions will help you write the Part B essay in which you will be asked:

> • In the early 1800s, Americans felt a growing sense of pride in their new nation. How did this feeling help Americans define their identity as a people? What obstacles did they face in developing this national identity?

Part A: Short-Answer Questions
Directions: Analyze the documents, and answer the short-answer questions that follow.

Document 1 John Adams, describing a meeting with a foreign ambassador, in his diary (1785)

> One of the foreign ambassadors said to me, "You have been often in England." "Never, but once in November and December, 1783." "You have relations in England, no doubt." "None at all." "None, how can that be? You are of English extraction!" "Neither my father or mother, grand-father or great grandmother, nor any other relation that I know of, or care a [cent] for, has been in England these one hundred and fifty years; so that you see I have not one drop of blood in my veins but what is American."

1. What country was the ambassador trying to link Adams with? _____
   _____
   _____

2. Why did Adams reject the ambassador's effort to link him with that country?
   _____
   _____

3. How does the conversation reveal Adams's sense of national pride? _____
   _____
   _____

Name _____ Class _____ Date _____

The Early Republic

Document 2 James Madison, writing about a problem that he worried might weaken the new government (1787)

> All civilized societies are divided into different interests . . . [such as] creditors or debtors, rich or poor—[farmers], merchants or manufacturers—members of different religious sects—followers of different leaders—owners of different kinds of property, etc., etc. In republican government, the majority . . . give the law. Whenever, therefore, a [shared] interest or common [goal] unites a majority, what is to [stop] them from unjust violations of the rights and interests of the minority?

4. What kinds of divisions does Madison see in society? _____

_____

_____

5. In a republic like the United States, how are laws made? _____

_____

_____

6. What problem does Madison worry might occur? _____

_____

_____

Document 3 Thomas Jefferson, giving instructions to Meriwether Lewis for his and William Clark's journey of exploration, in a letter (1803)

> The [goal] of your [journey] is to explore the Missouri river, [and] such [major] streams of it, as, by its course [and] communication with the waters of the Pacific Ocean, may offer the most direct [and useful] water [route] across this continent for the purposes of [trade]. . . .
>
> Your observations are to be taken with great pains [and] accuracy, to be entered [carefully] [and] intelligibly for others as well as yourself. . . . Other objects worthy of notice will be the soil and face of the country, its [plants] . . . the animals of the country . . . the mineral productions of every kind . . . climate of every kind. . . . In all your [meetings] with [Native Americans,] treat them in the most friendly . . . manner which their own conduct will admit.

7. What were the chief goals of Lewis and Clark's journey? _____

_____

_____

8. What kinds of records were Lewis and Clark instructed to keep?

_____

_____

The Early Republic·

Document 4   Painting showing British troops burning Washington, D.C., during the War of 1812

Courtesy of the Library of Congress

9. What are the people in the lower-right corner doing? _____

_____

_____

10. Who are the people in the lower-left corner? _____

_____

_____

11. What feelings does the artist express about the burning of Washington? Explain.

_____

_____

Document 5   Samuel Crabtree, writing to his brother in England about what he found after arriving in the United States, in a letter (1818)

> This is the country for a man to enjoy himself: Ohio, Indiana, and the Missouri Territory. . . .
>
> There is enough to spare of everything a person can desire; [I] have not heard either man or woman speak a word against the government or the price of [food and other supplies].
>
> The poorest families adorn the table three times a day like a wedding dinner. . . . Say, is it so in England?
>
> If you knew the difference between this country and England you would need no persuading to leave it and come hither.

12. What region of the United States does Crabtree describe? _____

_____

_____

13. What advantages does Crabtree see in moving to the United States? _____

_____

_____

14. What does Crabtree's letter suggest about life in England at the time?

_____

_____

Document 6   Engraving showing slaves loading cotton onto a steamboat in Mississippi (1820–1840)

North Wind Picture Archives

15. Who is shown in the engraving, and what are they doing? _____

_____

16. How does the engraving show differences between slaves and white workers in the South? _____

_____

The Early Republic

Document 7   Print showing mule barges on the Erie Canal (1825)

17. Why were mules used on the Erie Canal? _____

_____

_____

18. How does the print show that the canal changed the landscape?

_____

_____

_____

19. How does the print show that building the canal was a large undertaking?

_____

_____

_____

The Early Republic

Document 8   Reformer Frances Wright, arguing for changes to American society, in a speech (1829)

> The great [ideas written] in America's Declaration of Independence are true, are great, are [beautiful], and are *all her own*. But her . . . law, her religion, her education are false, narrow, prejudiced, ignorant, and are the relic of dark ages—the gift . . . of king-governed, priest-ridden nations, whose [rule] the people of America have . . . overthrown, but whose example they are still following. . . .
>
> The [change begun] at the Revolution of '76 has been but little improved through the . . . years [that followed]. . . . The national policy of the country was then indeed changed but . . . its social economy has remained such as it was in the days of . . . European [control].

20. What features of American society did Wright want changed? _____

_____

_____

_____

21. Why does Wright think that the Revolution of '76 was incomplete? _____

_____

_____

_____

22. How do Wright's comments reflect a sense of nationalism? _____

_____

_____

_____

Part B: Essay
Directions: Write a well-organized essay that includes an introduction, several paragraphs, and a conclusion. Use evidence from at least four documents in the body of the essay. Support your response with relevant facts, examples, and details. Include additional outside information.

> • In the early 1800s, Americans felt a growing sense of pride in their new nation. How did this feeling help Americans define their identity as a people? What obstacles did they face in developing this national identity?

An Era of Expansion

Part I: Multiple-Choice Questions

Identify the number of the choice that best completes the statement or answers the question.

_____ 1. What conclusion did President Andrew Jackson draw about the Bank of the United States?

    (1) It helped farmers and laborers.

    (2) It was controlled by states' rights supporters.

    (3) It helped mostly the wealthy.

    (4) It was controlled by foreign powers.

_____ 2. How were voting rights affected by growing democratic values in the 1820s?

    (1) Increasing numbers of people participated in the voting process.

    (2) Women gained the right to vote.

    (3) Voting rights were no longer determined by race.

    (4) Servants gained the right to vote.

_____ 3. Which of the following groups thought of Andrew Jackson as their champion?

    (1) merchants in New England

    (2) Native Americans in the North

    (3) common people across the country

    (4) wealthy planters in the South

_____ 4. Which statement about the 1824 presidential election is TRUE?

    (1) John Quincy Adams won the popular vote, and he became President.

    (2) Andrew Jackson won the popular vote, and he became President.

    (3) The House of Representatives chose John Quincy Adams as President.

    (4) The House of Representatives chose Andrew Jackson as President.

_____ 5. What contributed to the temporary peace between political parties in the 1820s?

    (1) the reconciliation between John Quincy Adams and Andrew Jackson

    (2) the new process of choosing presidential candidates

    (3) the founding of the Whig party

    (4) the disappearance of the Federalist party

_____ 6. Why was John Quincy Adams an unpopular President?

    (1) He favored the South over other regions.

    (2) He vetoed programs aimed at making internal improvements.

    (3) He forced Native Americans to leave their homelands.

    (4) He wanted to increase federal government spending.

An Era of Expansion

_____ 7. Which was a characteristic of the new politics reflected in the campaign of 1840?
  (1) Candidates focused on their war records to appeal to voters.
  (2) Both parties cooperated in the interest of national unity.
  (3) Both parties competed for voters by holding rallies.
  (4) Neither party engaged in mudslinging.

_____ 8. An agricultural economy developed in the South because
  (1) planters could raise crops at low costs.
  (2) the land and climate were ideal for cotton, rice, and livestock.
  (3) southerners wanted to live on estates like European royalty did.
  (4) other United States climates were not as well suited for agriculture.

_____ 9. All the following are methods that African Americans used to resist slavery EXCEPT
  (1) becoming skilled artisans.
  (2) trying to escape to the North.
  (3) breaking tools and destroying crops.
  (4) participating in slave revolts.

_____ 10. By 1860, free African Americans in the South
  (1) had the same rights as poor whites.
  (2) could travel throughout the South.
  (3) faced harsh discrimination.
  (4) made up one-third of the South's population.

_____ 11. What was the primary purpose of the slave codes?
  (1) to recognize slave marriages
  (2) to guarantee good working conditions for slaves
  (3) to prevent slaves from running away
  (4) to prevent slaves from practicing their religion

_____ 12. How did the high protective tariff of 1828 affect southern planters?
  (1) It protected them from foreign competition.
  (2) It increased the cost of European imports.
  (3) It increased their reliance on goods from the North.
  (4) It protected their land from migrating Native Americans.

_____ 13. Which of the following is one cause of the Panic of 1837?
  (1) the election of President Martin Van Buren
  (2) the Seminole Wars
  (3) the lack of paper money printed to meet the public demand
  (4) the large sums of money that speculators borrowed from banks

An Era of Expansion

_____ **14.** Which of the following occurred during Martin Van Buren's presidency?
   (1) Cotton prices rose, and southern planters prospered.
   (2) Factory production increased, and manufacturers prospered.
   (3) Unemployment fell when thousands of new jobs were created.
   (4) The nation suffered through a three-year depression.

_____ **15.** What was the BIGGEST threat to those who traveled west in wagon trains?
   (1) illnesses such as cholera   **(3)** lack of leadership
   (2) midwinter snowstorms   **(4)** overcrowded trails

_____ **16.** What led settlers and trappers to move to Oregon and the Far West in the 1820s?
   (1) the absence of Native Americans in the region
   (2) the lure of fertile lands, plentiful rainfall, and a mild climate
   (3) offers of jobs in the shipbuilding industry along the Oregon coast
   (4) the discovery of gold in the Willamette Valley

_____ **17.** How did the United States and Britain settle their dispute over Oregon?
   (1) The United States seized the land with military force.
   (2) The United States and Britain agreed to divide the land.
   (3) The United States bought the territory from Britain.
   (4) Britain bought the territory from the United States.

_____ **18.** Why did the Mormons move west to settle in Utah?
   (1) They sought gold.
   (2) They sought jobs on the railroads.
   (3) They hoped to escape religious persecution.
   (4) They wanted to convert Native Americans to Christianity.

_____ **19.** Mexicans influenced American culture in the Southwest by
   (1) teaching Americans new irrigation techniques and mining skills.
   (2) changing Americans' views about Manifest Destiny.
   (3) teaching Americans how to hunt in the desert.
   (4) persuading Americans to free their slaves.

_____ **20.** Why did American settlers in Texas come into conflict with Mexico in the 1830s?
   (1) Mexican laws prevented settlers from becoming Mexican citizens.
   (2) Mexico wanted to sell Texas to Spain.
   (3) Mexico feared losing Texas to the United States.
   (4) Settlers wanted to throw out the Mexican constitution.

An Era of Expansion

_____ **21.** What was one challenge faced by the "Lone Star Republic"?

(1) American and German settlers fought over the issue of slavery.

(2) The United States refused to recognize its independence.

(3) Large numbers of settlers left the republic.

(4) Mexico refused to recognize its independence.

_____ **22.** What final incident caused President Polk to urge Congress to declare war on Mexico?

(1) The United States annexed Texas.

(2) Mexico rejected President Polk's offer to buy California and New Mexico.

(3) American and Mexican troops clashed near the Rio Grande.

(4) The United Stares expanded to the Pacific Ocean.

_____ **23.** Which of the following led some people in BOTH the North and the South to oppose the abolition of slavery?

(1) They feared that former slaves would demand the same rights that white people had.

(2) They saw abolition as a threat to their economic livelihood.

(3) They feared that former slaves would demand education.

(4) They thought that freed slaves would burden the economy with unemployed workers.

_____ **24.** Which of the following BEST identifies a pioneering achievement of Elizabeth Blackwell?

(1) She was a powerful speaker against slavery.

(2) She opened a high school for girls.

(3) She became a licensed doctor.

(4) She became an elementary school teacher.

_____ **25.** Which of the following statements describes women's situation in the United States in the 1800s?

(1) An unmarried woman had no right to own property.

(2) A working woman's wages belonged to her husband.

(3) A woman could become a United States senator.

(4) A married woman could not work outside her home.

_____ **26.** Which of the following resolutions of the Seneca Falls Convention was barely passed?

(1) women's right to make public speeches

(2) women's right to own property

(3) women's right to hold public office

(4) women's right to vote

_____ **27.** How did the Second Great Awakening encourage the spread of social reform?

    (1) Its doctrine taught people to rely on society to solve their problems.

    (2) Its stress on the acceptance of differences led to the growth of many new religions.

    (3) Its stress on self-improvement led to a wish to improve the whole society.

    (4) Its doctrine encouraged the acceptance of female religious leaders.

_____ **28.** Which of the following was an accomplishment of educational reformers in the 1800s?

    (1) Colleges were created for people with disabilities.

    (2) Public high schools were built in most northern states.

    (3) Public elementary schools were built in most northern states.

    (4) African American and white students attended the same schools in most states.

_____ **29.** What was a central influence on the styles of American painters before 1800?

    (1) frontier life   **(3)** the abolition of slavery

    (2) European painting traditions   **(4)** the growth of the city

_____ **30.** Which of the following was a result of Dorothea Dix's efforts at social reform?

    (1) States banned the sale of alcohol.

    (2) Children were released from prison.

    (3) Mental illness was treated as a minor crime.

    (4) Insanity was treated as an illness, not a crime.

_____ **31.** Which of the following themes was common in the poetry of Walt Whitman?

    (1) temperance   **(3)** predestination

    (2) prison reform   **(4)** democracy

_____ **32.** What did temperance groups view as the most serious social problem of the 1800s?

    (1) lack of religious faith   **(3)** overcrowded schools

    (2) alcohol abuse   **(4)** shortage of mental hospitals

_____ **33.** Which statement BEST illustrates the South's dependence on the North?

    (1) Northern manufacturers borrowed money from southern banks to buy raw materials.

    (2) Northerners bought manufactured goods from southern factories.

    (3) Southern planters borrowed money from northern banks to buy farm tools.

    (4) Southerners relied on northern factory models.

An Era of Expansion

Part II: Constructed-Response Question

DIRECTIONS: *Answer the questions that follow the written document using the space provided. Base your answers to questions 1, 2, and 3 on the reading below and on your knowledge of social studies.*

I lived in the family of Master Hugh, at Baltimore, seven years. . . . My mistress—who had begun to teach me—was suddenly checked in [this kind action], by the strong advice of her husband. . . . Mrs. Auld . . . set out, when I first went to live with her, to treat me as she supposed one human being ought to treat another.

. . . One cannot easily forget to love freedom: and it is as hard to cease to respect that natural love in our fellow creatures. On entering upon the career of a slaveholding mistress, Mrs. Auld was [particularly lacking]: nature, which fits nobody for such an office, had done less for her than any lady I had known. It was no easy matter to induce her to think and to feel that the curly-headed boy, who stood by her side, and even leaned on her lap; who was loved by little Tommy, and who loved little Tommy in turn; sustained to her only the relation of [a piece of property]. I was *more* than that, and she felt me to be more than that. . . . I was human, and she, dear lady, knew and felt me to be so. How could she, then, treat me as a brute, without a mighty struggle with all the noble powers of her own soul.

—*Frederick Douglass (1817?–1895)*

Source: Frederick Douglass, *My Bondage and My Freedom*, edited by William Andrews. Chicago: University of Illinois Press, 1988.

1. Why did Mrs. Auld stop teaching young Frederick Douglass to read and write?

_____

_____

2. According to Douglass, what conflict did Mrs. Auld face? _____

_____

_____

3. How did Frederick Douglass and other abolitionists help the antislavery movement?

_____

_____

_____

An Era of Expansion

Part III: Document-Based Question

Theme: Expansion

This question is based on the accompanying documents (1–8). This question is designed to test your ability to work with historical documents. Some of the documents have been edited for the purposes of the question. As you analyze the documents, take into account the source of each document and any point of view that may be presented in the document.

Historical Context:
Conflicts as well as successes characterized the expansion of the United States from 1820 to 1860.

Task:
Using information from the documents and your knowledge of social studies, answer the questions that follow each document in Part A. Your answers to the questions will help you write the Part B essay in which you will be asked:

> • In the years from 1820 to 1860, the United States grew to stretch "from sea to shining sea." What were some key developments that made this growth possible? What problems resulted from this rapid and massive expansion?

Part A: Short-Answer Questions
Directions: Analyze the documents, and answer the short-answer questions that follow.

Document 1 John Louis O'Sullivan, describing the nation's destiny to grow, in an editorial in the *New York Morning News* (1845)

> Our manifest destiny [is] to overspread and to possess the whole of the continent which [God] has given us for the development of the great experiment of liberty and federated self-government entrusted to us.

1. What is "the great experiment of liberty" that O'Sullivan mentions?

   _____

   _____

2. What phrase did O'Sullivan use to describe the drive to expand, and what did he mean? _____

   _____

3. How did O'Sullivan make the drive to expand sound like a noble goal?

   _____

   _____

Document 2 Cherokee women, urging resistance to the United States government plan to move their people west, in a petition (1818)

> We have heard with painful feelings that the bounds of the land we now possess are to be drawn into very narrow limits. The land was given to us

by the Great Spirit above as our common right, to raise our children upon.
. . . We, therefore, humbly petition . . . the head men of warriors, to hold
out to the last in support of our common rights, as the Cherokee nations
have been the first settlers of this land. . . . [We] claim the right of the soil.

4. Why were the Cherokee women motivated to write this petition? _____

_____

_____

5. How do the Cherokee women justify their claim to the land? _____

_____

_____

6. What do the Cherokee women want their men to do? _____

_____

_____

Document 3 Noah Smithwick, remembering why he had decided to move to Texas in
1827, in his memoir *The Evolution of a State* (1900)

Sterling C. Robinson, who had obtained a grant for a colony, . . . went up into
Kentucky recruiting [settlers]. The glowing terms in which he talked of the
advantages to be gained by [moving to Texas] were well calculated to further
his scheme. To every head of a family, if a farmer, was promised 177 acres of
farming land and 4,428 acres of pasture land for stock; colonists [were] to be
exempt from taxation six years from date of settlement, with the privilege of
importing, duty free, everything they might desire for themselves and families; [and] an abundance of game. . . . The climate was so mild that houses were
not essential. . . . Corn in any quantity was to be had for the planting.

7. How did Robinson make Texas sound attractive? _____

_____

_____

_____

8. What impact did Robinson's description have on Smithwick? How can you tell?

_____

_____

_____

Document 4 Mexican historian Justo Sierra, writing about events just before the
Mexican War, in *The Mexican War: Was It Manifest Destiny?* (1963)

In the sphere of international law [Mexican] diplomacy constantly got
the better of the American. This was shown in the conferences that took

An Era of Expansion

place between the United States and Mexico to settle claims [over boundaries]. . . . [It was also seen in] the [calm] notes with which Mexico called attention to the series of [insults] permitted by the Washington government against the dignity of the Mexican Republic.

. . . Even if the right of annexation could be claimed by Texans, it could only be claimed by [the United States] by first settling the [other] issues with [Mexico].

9. How does Sierra compare Mexican diplomacy to American diplomacy?

_____

_____

10. How does this historian view the behavior of the United States toward Mexico?

_____

_____

11. Does Sierra approve of the annexation of Texas? Explain your answer.

_____

_____

Document 5 Chinese folk song (1850s), supposedly sung by wives whose husbands left to work in the United States

Right after we were wed, Husband, you set
out on a journey.
How was I to tell you how I felt?
Wandering around a foreign country, when
will you ever come home?
I beg of you, after you depart, to come back soon,
Our separation will be only a flash of time;
I only wish that you would have good fortune,
In three years you would be home again.
Also, I beg of you that your heart won't change,
That you keep your heart and mind on taking care
of your family;
Each month or half a month send a letter home,
In two or three years my wish is to welcome you home.

12. How did Chinese women feel about their husbands leaving for the United States?

_____

13. What hopes and fears did the women have? _____

_____

14. How is this song useful as a primary source? _____

_____

An Era of Expansion

Document 6   Unnamed author describing gold-mining activity in California, in a newspaper story in the *San Francisco Californian* (1848)

> There are now about four thousand white persons, besides a number of Indians engaged at the mines, and from the fact, that no capital is required, they are working in companies on equal shares or alone with their basket. In one part of the mine called the "dry digins," no other implements are necessary than an ordinary sheath knife, to pick the gold from the rocks. In other parts, where the gold is washed out, the machinery is very simple. . . . [By] far the largest number use nothing but a large tin pan or an Indian basket, into which they place the dirt and shake it until the gold gets to the bottom.

15. What kinds of technology and skills did the early Gold Rush miners have?

_____

_____

16. How did newspaper stories like this one attract people to California? _____

_____

17. What view of the Gold Rush does the author present? _____

_____

_____

Document 7   Photograph showing a pioneer family in Michigan (1850s)

Clarke Historical Library, Central Michigan University

18. How does this photograph reveal the work required to make a home in the

wilderness? _____

_____

An Era of Expansion

19. How did pioneer families like this change the landscape on the frontier?

_____

_____

20. Does the photograph seem to favor or oppose such expansion? Explain your answer.

_____

_____

Document 8 Abigail Scott Duniway, describing the move west by her cousin's family, in a letter to her grandfather (1852)

> [The family was in] a heavy wagon without springs, [covered] by strong canvas stretched smoothly over bows of new hickory, drawn together in a circle at the rear by a strong cord and [tied] to the front. . . . A rifle, [hinting at] possible [meetings] with Indians, hung from a leather strap against the [front] on one side. . . . The wagon bed was packed with boxes and bundles neatly stored. . . . A low chair, sitting sideways, with barely room in front to place the feet, [was used] by the babe, when tired, as a place to sit, the mother [moving out of the way] at the expense of her own comfort.
>
> Thus equipped, a weak woman with her babe started on a transcontinental journey of between 2000 and 3000 miles, across mountains, streams and arid plains. . . . In this wagon she lived and journeyed patiently, even cheerfully.

21. Based on the document, what kinds of equipment did settlers take on their move west? _____

_____

22. What hardships did they face on the journey west? _____

_____

_____

23. How does Duniway reveal her attitude toward her cousin's family? _____

_____

_____

Part B: Essay
Directions: Write a well-organized essay that includes an introduction, several paragraphs, and a conclusion. Use evidence from at least four documents in the body of the essay. Support your response with relevant facts, examples, and details. Include additional outside information.

- In the years from 1820 to 1860, the United States grew to stretch "from sea to shining sea." What were some key developments that made this growth possible? What problems resulted from this rapid and massive expansion?

Division and Reunion

Part I: Multiple-Choice Questions

Identify the number of the choice that best completes the statement or answers the question.

_____ 1. Which of the following political parties was formed in 1848 for the purpose of banning slavery in western territories?
(1) Democrat
(3) Whig
(2) Free-Soil
(4) Republican

_____ 2. Which statement summarizes the effects of the Missouri Compromise?
(1) It had little effect on the balance of slave and free states.
(2) It helped ensure a balance of slave and free states for almost thirty years.
(3) It triggered a sharp rise in the number of free states shortly after 1848.
(4) It ensured a decrease in the number of slave states.

_____ 3. Which of the following is NOT among the terms of the Compromise of 1850?
(1) Slavery is banned in New Mexico and Utah.
(2) Northerners are required to help return runaway slaves to owners.
(3) The slave trade is outlawed in Washington, D.C.
(4) A border dispute between Texas and New Mexico is settled.

_____ 4. Which of the following is an example of *popular sovereignty*?
(1) In 1837, Michigan becomes a free state because it is north of Missouri.
(2) In 1836, Arkansas becomes a slave state because it is south of Missouri.
(3) In 1849, California voters approve a state constitution that bans slavery.
(4) In 1846, the House of Representatives bans slavery in territories won from Mexico.

_____ 5. What led to the violence in Kansas in 1855?
(1) the repeal of the Compromise of 1850
(2) the election of Abraham Lincoln as President
(3) the verdict in *Dred Scott* v. *Sandford*
(4) the rivalry between proslavery and antislavery settlers

_____ 6. What effect did *Uncle Tom's Cabin* have on public opinion?
(1) Northerners, in general, became more sympathetic toward slave owners.
(2) Northerners, in general, became more opposed to slavery.
(3) Southerners, in general, began to see slavery as a moral evil.
(4) Americans, in general, lost interest in the slavery issue.

_____ 7. Which of the following led to the formation of the Republican party in the 1850s?
(1) belief in the need for stronger support for the Fugitive Slave Act
(2) dissatisfaction with how the Whigs dealt with protective tariffs
(3) dissatisfaction with the weak stand on slavery taken by the Whigs and Democrats
(4) belief that the western territories needed more representation

Division and Reunion

_____ **8.** How did the ruling in the *Dred Scott* case affect the slavery debate?
  (1) It protected the right of a freed slave to file a lawsuit.
  (2) It determined the authority of Congress to outlaw slavery in territories.
  (3) It temporarily united antislavery and proslavery forces.
  (4) It reversed the Missouri Compromise.

_____ **9.** Which of the following can be said of Abraham Lincoln?
  (1) His military accomplishments made him a national hero.
  (2) His debates with Stephen Douglas won him fame as an opponent of slavery.
  (3) His antislavery speeches won him a following in both the North and the South.
  (4) His support for the Kansas-Nebraska Act made him a Republican leader.

_____ **10.** What effect did Abraham Lincoln's election in 1860 have on national unity?
  (1) It healed the nation's political divisions.
  (2) South Carolina seceded, but other southern states remained in the Union.
  (3) Several southern states seceded in protest.
  (4) It caused the South to declare war on the North.

_____ **11.** Which statement summarizes the outcome of the presidential election of 1860?
  (1) Overwhelming support from southern voters carried Abraham Lincoln to victory.
  (2) Abraham Lincoln won despite the fact that he did not carry even one southern state.
  (3) Moderates helped Abraham Lincoln carry enough southern states to win.
  (4) Abraham Lincoln won with strong support in every region of the country.

_____ **12.** How did the Civil War begin?
  (1) Federal troops attacked Fort Sumter, South Carolina.
  (2) Confederate troops attacked Fort Sumter, South Carolina
  (3) Confederate troops attacked federal forts off the coast of Florida.
  (4) Union troops attacked Confederate forts off the coast of Florida.

_____ **13.** Which of the following was a successful strategy for wining the Civil War?
  (1) The Confederacy prolonged fighting until the northern spirit broke.
  (2) The Union pursued the Confederates back to the South after the Battle of Antietam.
  (3) The Union took control of the Mississippi River.
  (4) The Confederacy continued to receive supplies from Europe.

_____ **14.** What was the North's one official goal at the start of the Civil War?
  (1) to protect the northern way of life
  (2) to abolish slavery
  (3) to drive slave states out of the Union
  (4) to keep the Union together

_____ **15.** What was one effect of the Emancipation Proclamation?
  (1) It caused many European nations to come to the aid of the Confederacy.
  (2) It added the abolition of slavery in the South to the Union's war goals.
  (3) It changed northern strategy from an offensive to a defensive plan.
  (4) It ended slavery in the Union.

_____ **16.** Early Civil War battles showed
  (1) the need for well-trained soldiers.
  (2) the lack of civilian support for the Confederate war effort.
  (3) the strength of Union military leadership.
  (4) the likely Confederate victory in the war.

_____ **17.** How did the South deal with economic problems during the war?
  (1) President Davis increased cotton shipments to Britain.
  (2) Plantations grew food crops.
  (3) The government cut prices so that people could afford to buy goods.
  (4) The government issued bonds.

_____ **18.** Which of these individuals was the president of the Confederacy during the Civil War?
  (1) Robert E. Lee   **(3)** Abraham Lincoln
  (2) Jefferson Davis   **(4)** Ulysses S. Grant

_____ **19.** How did African Americans in the Union army contribute to the war effort?
  (1) They fought alongside white soldiers from the beginning.
  (2) They served only as laborers throughout the war.
  (3) They fought in major battles by 1863.
  (4) They worked mostly in gun factories.

_____ **20.** Which of the following individuals served as a Confederate nurse during the Civil War?
  (1) Sojourner Truth   **(3)** Clara Barton
  (2) Sally Tompkins   **(4)** Dorothea Dix

_____ **21.** What is one problem that northerners faced during the war?
  (1) Certain rights were suspended to preserve public safety.
  (2) Congress refused to approve an income tax to pay for the war.
  (3) Farm production decreased steadily.
  (4) Women refused to work in the factories.

_____ **22.** How did Ulysses S. Grant's concept of total war differ from earlier strategies?
  (1) Civilians and their property were left untouched.
  (2) Civilians were subject to the same hardships as enemy soldiers.
  (3) The army and the navy attacked enemy strongholds together.
  (4) No prisoners were taken.

Division and Reunion

_____ **23.** Which of the following was a major result of the Civil War?
  (1) The Democrats became the dominant political party.
  (2) The bonds linking the states were loosened.
  (3) The federal government became weaker.
  (4) Slavery was ended everywhere in the United States.

_____ **24.** How did MOST freedmen meet their basic needs after the Civil War ended?
  (1) They returned to the land where they had worked as slaves.
  (2) They received "40 acres and a mule."
  (3) They opened small businesses.
  (4) They owned their own land through sharecropping.

_____ **25.** After President Lincoln was reelected, he stated that his major goal was to
  (1) call a truce.
  (2) continue to fight until slavery was abolished.
  (3) work toward peace and unity.
  (4) punish the South after the war.

_____ **26.** Which statement BEST summarizes early Reconstruction efforts?
  (1) Congress agreed to support Lincoln's Ten Percent Plan.
  (2) Lincoln signed the Wade-Davis Bill into law.
  (3) Lincoln signed a bill establishing the Freedmen's Bureau.
  (4) Congress overrode Lincoln's veto of the black codes.

_____ **27.** What state laws unfairly used economic status to deny African Americans their right to vote?
  (1) grandfather clauses   **(3)** Jim Crow laws
  (2) poll taxes   **(4)** literacy tests

_____ **28.** How did members of Congress react to the black codes?
  (1) Most representatives believed that the black codes were fair and just.
  (2) Outraged Republicans vowed to develop a stricter Reconstruction plan.
  (3) Congress used the black codes as a model for a new Reconstruction plan.
  (4) Northern representatives argued that the black codes were an issue for each state to decide.

_____ **29.** Radical Republicans gained power in Congress by
  (1) joining forces with moderate Republicans to reduce the power of southern Democrats.
  (2) promising to rebuild the South.
  (3) promising to enforce the black codes.
  (4) joining forces with moderate Republicans to pass the Thirteenth Amendment.

_____ **30.** Which group was NOT among the new forces in southern politics after the Civil War?
  (1) white Republicans   **(3)** African Americans
  (2) white Conservatives   **(4)** transplanted northerners

Division and Reunion

_____ **31.** Why did conflict erupt shortly after the assassination of President Lincoln?

    (1) Southern members of Congress pushed President Johnson's Radical Reconstruction plan.

    (2) Republicans disapproved of President Johnson's Reconstruction plan.

    (3) Republicans enacted the black codes against the wishes of southern members of Congress.

    (4) Southern members of Congress set up the Joint Committee on Reconstruction.

_____ **32.** Which of the following statements is TRUE of Reconstruction governments?

    (1) Corruption among state officials was rare during Reconstruction.

    (2) Reconstruction governments lowered state taxes.

    (3) Corruption among state officials angered white southerners.

    (4) Reconstruction governments neglected the education of white children.

_____ **33.** Why did Reconstruction governments increase taxes after the Civil War?

    (1) to punish the South for starting the Civil War

    (2) to cover the costs of rebuilding the North

    (3) to cover the costs of rebuilding the South

    (4) to cover mismanaged money spent by corrupt government officials

_____ **34.** Why did southern states agree to ratify the Thirteenth Amendment?

    (1) Ratification of the amendment helped their states win presidential approval to rejoin the Union.

    (2) The amendment called for a majority of white men in each state to swear loyalty to the United States.

    (3) The amendment banned slavery throughout the United States.

    (4) The amendment laid the foundation for the South's public school system.

_____ **35.** Which of the following helped bring about the end of Reconstruction?

    (1) the growing power of Radical Republicans

    (2) renewed southern threats to secede

    (3) stories of corruption in Grant's administration

    (4) reforms put in place by southern conservatives

_____ **36.** How did the South develop its industries after the Civil War?

    (1) It imported resources such as lumber and iron ore from Europe.

    (2) It relied on the North to supply natural resources for making steel.

    (3) It developed its own natural resources for making clothing.

    (4) It developed steel instead of agricultural products such as cotton and tobacco.

_____ **37.** Why did sharecroppers become trapped in a cycle of poverty?

    (1) They did not understand farming.

    (2) Prices for farm products fell during Reconstruction.

    (3) They did not earn enough cash to pay their debts.

    (4) State laws prevented sharecroppers from owning land.

Division and Reunion

Part II: Constructed-Response Question

DIRECTIONS: *Answer the questions that follow the written document using the space provided. Base your answers to questions 1, 2, and 3 on the reading and on your knowledge of social studies.*

Date	Legislation	Purpose
1865	13th Amendment	• Abolishes slavery
1865, 1866	Freedman's Bureau	• Provides services for newly freed people
1867	Reconstruction Acts	• Establishes Republican Reconstruction program
1868	14th Amendment	• Defines citizenship to include African Americans
1870	15th Amendment	• Guarantees equal protection under the law • Guarantees voting rights
1875	Civil Rights Act	• Protects rights of African Americans in public places

1. Based on the chart, what are three rights that African Americans gained during Reconstruction? _____

   _____

   _____

2. Which pieces of legislation were designed to guarantee African Americans not only the right, but the ability to participate in civic life? _____

   _____

   _____

3. How did this legislation reflect basic American values, beliefs, and traditions in important historic documents like the Declaration of Independence and Constitution?

   _____

   _____

   _____

Division and Reunion

Part III: Document-Based Question

Theme: Sectionalism

This question is based on the accompanying documents (1–9). This question is designed to test your ability to work with historical documents. Some of the documents have been edited for the purposes of the question. As you analyze the documents, take into account the source of each document and any point of view that may be presented in the document.

Historical Context:
From 1820 to 1860, in an increasingly bitter debate, the North and South divided over the issue of slavery and its spread into the territories.

Task:
Using information from the documents and your knowledge of social studies, answer the questions that follow each document in Part A. Your answers to the questions will help you write the Part B essay in which you will be asked:

> • In the early 1800s, the North and South developed different economies and social institutions. One key difference was the presence or absence of slavery. How did the two sections address the issue of slavery before, during, and after the Civil War?

Part A: Short-Answer Questions
Directions: Analyze the documents, and answer the short-answer questions that follow.

Document 1   Angelina Grimké, urging southern women to fight against slavery, in a pamphlet that was banned in the South (1836)

> I have . . . clearly proved . . . that slavery is contrary to our declaration of independence. [I have also shown] that it is contrary to the first charter of human rights given to Adam. . . . [I have also shown] that slavery in America reduces a *man* to a *thing*, . . . *robs him* of *all* his rights as a *human being.* . . .
>
> But perhaps you will be ready to [ask], why appeal to *women* on this subject? . . . You can do much in every way: four things I will name. [First,] you can read on this subject. [Second,] you can pray over this subject. [Third,] you can speak on this subject. [Fourth,] you can *act* on this subject.

1. What arguments does Grimké make against slavery? _____

_____

_____

2. Why does she think that women can bring about change? _____

_____

_____

Division and Reunion

3. Why would officials in the South ban the pamphlet? _____

_____

_____

Document 2 Representative Robert Toombs of Georgia, arguing against a proposed law that would have banned slavery from land obtained as a result of the Mexican War, in a speech in Congress (1849)

> If by your legislation you seek to drive us from the territories of California and New Mexico, purchased by the common blood and treasure of the whole people, . . . *I am for disunion.* . . . From 1787 to this hour the people of the South have asked nothing but justice. . . . The Territories are the common property of the people of the United States. . . . It is [House members'] duty . . . to remove all [barriers] to the free enjoyment [of the territories] by all . . . people of the union, the slaveholder and the nonslaveholder.

4. What threat does Toombs make? _____

_____

5. What arguments does Toombs use to support his call to allow slavery in the

territories? _____

_____

6. How does Toombs try to appeal to all Americans? _____

_____

_____

Document 3 Senator William H. Seward of New York, arguing against approval of the Compromise of 1850, in a Senate speech (1850)

> I am opposed to any such compromise, in any and all the forms in which it has been proposed. . . . [The] simple, bold, and even awful question which presents itself to us, is this: shall we establish [slavery] or permit it . . . to be established? Sir, our forefathers would not have hesitated an hour. . . . The most alarming evidence of our [moral decline], which has yet been given, is found in the fact that we even debate such a question.

7. Why did Seward oppose compromise?_____

_____

8. How did stands like Seward's make compromise harder to achieve?

_____

_____

Division and Reunion

Document 4 Abolitionist poster warning African Americans in the North that under the Fugitive Slave Law they could be captured and taken South (1851)

CAUTION!!

COLORED PEOPLE

OF BOSTON, ONE & ALL,

You are hereby respectfully CAUTIONED and advised, to avoid conversing with the

Watchmen and Police Officers of Boston,

For since the recent ORDER OF THE MAYOR & ALDERMEN, they are empowered to act as

KIDNAPPERS

AND

Slave Catchers,

And they have already been actually employed in KIDNAPPING, CATCHING, AND KEEPING SLAVES. Therefore, if you value your LIBERTY, and the *Welfare of the Fugitives* among you, *Shun* them in every possible manner, as so many *HOUNDS* on the track of the most unfortunate of your race.

Keep a Sharp Look Out for KIDNAPPERS, and have TOP EYE open.

APRIL 24, 1851.

9. Why does this poster compare the police to "kidnappers"? _____

_____

_____

10. How was this poster designed to influence public opinion? _____

_____

_____

11. What was the general message of this poster? _____

_____

_____

Division and Reunion

Document 5 Photograph showing a group of antislavery settlers in Kansas ready to fight against proslavery forces (1856)

12. How does the photograph show these men's determination? _____

_____

_____

_____

13. How does the photograph show the failure of compromise in Kansas?

_____

_____

_____

Division and Reunion

Document 6   Table comparing the number of casualties during the Civil War

	North	**South**
Killed in action or mortally wounded	110,100	94,000
Died of disease	224,580	164,000
Died as prisoners of war	30,192	31,000
Nonbattle deaths	24,881	not known
Wounded in action	275,175	194,026

Source: *Brother Against Brother,* © 1990 Time-Life Books, Inc.

14. What was the major cause of death during the Civil War? _____

_____

_____

15. Which side suffered heavier casualties during the Civil War? Explain your answer.

_____

_____

16. What are two conclusions you can draw from this table? _____

_____

_____

Document 7   Photograph showing the ruins of Richmond, Virginia (1865)

The National Archives/Corbis

17. What does the photograph reveal about the destruction of Richmond?

_____

_____

18. What are some feelings the photograph might stir in viewers, and how was this done? _____

_____

19. What does the photograph suggest about the impact of the Civil War on the South?

_____

_____

Document 8   Henry Adams, explaining freedom to his former owner (1865)

> If I cannot do like a white man, I am not free. I see how the poor white people do. I ought to do so too, or else I am a slave.

20. What does Adams want? _____

_____

21. What conclusion might be drawn from this document about the goal of former slaves? _____

_____

Division and Reunion

Document 9 Photograph showing a northern abolitionist who taught in South Carolina along with some of her African American students (1866)

Photographs and Prints Division, Schomburg Center for Research in Black Culture, The New York Public Library, Astor, Lenox and Tilden Foundation

22. What is the relationship between teacher and students shown in the photograph?

_____

_____

23. Who might have been the audience for this photograph? Explain your answer.

_____

_____

Part B: Essay
Directions: Write a well-organized essay that includes an introduction, several paragraphs, and a conclusion. Use evidence from at least four documents in the body of the essay. Support your response with relevant facts, examples, and details. Include additional outside information.

> • In the early 1800s, the North and South developed different economies and social institutions. One key difference was the presence or absence of slavery. How did the two sections address the issue of slavery before, during, and after the Civil War?

Transforming the Nation

Part I: Multiple-Choice Questions

Identify the number of the choice that best completes the statement or answers the question.

_____ 1. What role did the buffalo play in the lives of Plains Indians?
  (1) They were the focus of the Plains Indians' religious beliefs.
  (2) They were captured and sold as livestock to farmers.
  (3) They were a source of food, clothing, tools, and shelter.
  (4) They were a source of income because Indians sold their meat to railroad workers.

_____ 2. Why did buffalo herds decline in the 1830s and 1840s?
  (1) increased numbers of Native American buffalo hunters
  (2) increased demand for buffalo meat in eastern restaurants
  (3) increased demand for water resources on the plains
  (4) increased market for buffalo robes

_____ 3. What were the terms of the Fort Laramie Treaty?
  (1) Land would be reserved for Native Americans forever, and they would receive tools, domestic animals, and money.
  (2) Native Americans would share the gold and silver found on their nations' lands.
  (3) Native American villages would not be attacked if they agreed to fly the American flag.
  (4) The government would ban buffalo hunting on Native American lands, if the Native Americans allowed mining.

_____ 4. At which of the following locations did Native Americans win a victory over cavalry troops?
  (1) Snake River Valley   (3) Little Big Horn Valley
  (2) Fort Laramie   (4) New Mexico desert

_____ 5. Why was the Dawes Act of 1887 unsuccessful?
  (1) Native Americans wanted to resettle on reservations.
  (2) White settlers were unwilling to sell land for the creation of reservations.
  (3) The act ignored the traditional Native American views of land ownership.
  (4) The act gave too much power to Native American leaders.

_____ 6. How did the Native American way of life come to an end?
  (1) The government took away the power of tribal leaders.
  (2) Many Native Americans migrated to other countries.
  (3) Native Americans abandoned their traditions in favor of European customs.
  (4) Native American leaders stopped teaching traditions to young people.

_____ 7. Which of the following posed the GREATEST threat to cowhands on cattle drives?
  (1) lack of food   (3) runaway herds
  (2) poor housing   (4) attacks from groups of vaqueros

Transforming the Nation

_____ **8.** Which of the following was the MAIN function of cow towns during the cattle boom?

(1) Their location linked the cattle trails with eastern markets.

(2) They attracted settlers who wanted to establish their religion in the West.

(3) They catered to cowhands who needed meals and boarding.

(4) Their factories manufactured barbed wire for farmers' fences.

_____ **9.** Why did many Exodusters move to Kansas in 1879?

(1) to take advantage of cheap labor on new railroad lines leading south to Texas

(2) to homestead new land because African Americans' rights were challenged at the end of Reconstruction

(3) to establish townships, transportation systems, and courts in rural areas of the new state

(4) to escape fierce competition for mining rights in Colorado, Wyoming, and California

_____ **10.** Which of the following presented the greatest challenge to Plains farmers in the 1800s?

(1) infertile soil

(2) inadequate housing

(3) lack of sufficient land area

(4) lack of farming technology

_____ **11.** Which of the following BEST describes a problem Plains farmers faced because of the climate?

(1) Summer flooding often destroyed crops.

(2) Harsh winter winds and deep snow trapped pioneers in their homes.

(3) Farmers had to break up tough sod using hand tools.

(4) Farmers rarely produced adequate harvests because of the short growing season.

_____ **12.** Which of the following practices led many small farmers to join the Populist party?

(1) Rival railroads slashed prices in areas where competition for customers was fierce.

(2) Railroad owners used rebates and pools to keep prices artificially high.

(3) Railroad companies consolidated to improve efficiency and lower costs.

(4) Railroad companies created special departments for shipping and accounting.

_____ **13.** What was the MOST significant effect of the gold and silver boom on development in the West?

(1) Most prospectors made large fortunes and established thriving communities.

(2) Boomtowns that went "bust" turned into ghost towns, and population decreased in the West.

(3) A "population boom" accompanied the mining boom.

(4) Most prospectors did not strike it rich and moved back East, depleting the West's population.

Transforming the Nation

_____ **14.** Which of the following problems were caused by the mining boom?
    (1) water pollution, loss of forests, overuse of grasslands
    (2) loss of forests, water pollution, racism
    (3) racism, water pollution, overuse of grasslands
    (4) overuse of grasslands, loss of forests, racism

_____ **15.** Which statement BEST exemplifies the impact of technology on economics in the late 1800s?
    (1) The tragedy at the Triangle Shirtwaist Factory led to improved worker safety laws.
    (2) Federal courts ruled that the Sherman Antitrust Act limited workers' right to strike.
    (3) Wages for workers declined as more factories used new machines to produce goods.
    (4) Union membership soared after the strike against the Missouri Pacific Railroad in 1885.

_____ **16.** Which advance made a network of railroad lines possible?
    (1) the air brake   **(3)** the convertible berth
    (2) a standard gauge   **(4)** the dining car

_____ **17.** Which of the following was NOT a factor in the growth of huge steel empires after the Civil War?
    (1) the railroads' need for strong, durable rails
    (2) the cost-cutting benefits of the Bessemer process
    (3) the growing popularity of skyscrapers in big cities
    (4) the development of a less-polluting manufacturing process

_____ **18.** Who laid an underwater cable that transmitted telegraph messages from North America to Europe?
    (1) Alexander Graham Bell   **(3)** Cyrus Field
    (2) Samuel Morse   **(4)** Thomas Edison

_____ **19.** Which of the following was NOT a problem that led workers to form labor organizations?
    (1) low wages   **(3)** unsafe working conditions
    (2) high unemployment rates   **(4)** use of child labor

_____ **20.** What strategy did John D. Rockefeller use to strengthen Standard Oil?
    (1) built his own steel mill
    (2) controlled most domestic oil production
    (3) refused to form corporations
    (4) forced railroads to give him rebates

_____ **21.** Which of the following inventions were developed by Thomas Edison?
    (1) typewriter, refrigerated rail car, automatic engine-oiling machine
    (2) motor-driven vacuum cleaner, cash register, milking machine
    (3) motion picture projector, electric power plant, phonograph
    (4) electric streetcar, passenger elevator brake, shoemaking machine

Transforming the Nation

_____ 22. Which of the following advances did women workers make during the late 1800s?
(1) Women became the leaders of the two largest labor unions.
(2) Women garment workers won better pay and shorter work hours.
(3) Women organizers successfully lobbied for laws prohibiting child labor.
(4) Women in all occupations won equal pay for equal work.

_____ 23. Which statement BEST explains how railroads affected the economy of the United States in the years following the Civil War?
(1) Railroad companies' unfair practices caused a general depression in the late 1860s.
(2) Railroad companies created thousands of jobs and pioneered new business practices.
(3) Railroad companies created monopolies that stalled the building of new tracks.
(4) Railroad companies received rebates that allowed small rail companies to survive.

_____ 24. Which statement BEST explains how banks contributed to the growth of the economy in the years after the Civil War?
(1) Banks lent millions of dollars to corporations.
(2) Banks gained control of major corporations.
(3) Banks adopted policies that reduced competition.
(4) Banks made huge profits in hard economic times.

_____ 25. Which statement BEST describes changing population patterns between 1860 and 1890?
(1) Many young Americans left big cities, and they moved to farms.
(2) Many African Americans moved from northern cities to the rural South.
(3) Most new immigrants to the United States settled in cities.
(4) Most new immigrants to the United States settled in the West, and they bought farms.

_____ 26. Which of the following inventions was NOT a result of the building boom in the late 1800s?
(1) subway
(2) carriage
(3) elevated railroad
(4) electric streetcar

_____ 27. How did the population increase during the building boom in the late 1800s affect city life?
(1) Urban parkland was used to build housing for the poor.
(2) Owners were required to add elevators to preexisting buildings.
(3) Department stores were moved to suburban locations.
(4) Skyscrapers were built to conserve space.

_____ 28. What was the most important effect of Henry Ford's method of automobile production?
(1) Manufacturers could produce more luxury cars for the wealthy.
(2) Millions of Americans could afford automobiles.
(3) Female workers were hired for factory work for the first time.
(4) Manufacturers produced cars with more mechanical defects.

_____ **29.** What led critics to complain about the types of stories covered in newspapers in the late 1800s?

(1) difficult reading levels   **(3)** too much local news

(2) yellow journalism   **(4)** color comics

_____ **30.** The Chinese Exclusion Act

(1) allowed the development of specific neighborhoods for immigrants.

(2) was the first law to prevent immigrants from practicing their religion.

(3) excluded a national group from working in certain parts of the United States.

(4) was the first law to prevent a national group from entering the United States.

_____ **31.** Which of the following had the strongest affect on the growth of public education after the Civil War?

(1) summer Bible camps

(2) manual training schools

(3) compulsory education laws

(4) parochial schools

_____ **32.** What German educational idea was widely adopted in the United States after 1873?

(1) high school   **(3)** one-room schoolhouse

(2) kindergarten   **(4)** college

_____ **33.** Which of the following belongs in a list of remedies that reformers used to solve city problems?

(1) professional fire companies   **(3)** tenement housing

(2) suburbs   **(4)** stricter immigration laws

_____ **34.** Which of the following describes a main theme found in realist writing in the late 1800s?

(1) the luxury of the wealthy   **(3)** the life of factory owners

(2) the glamour of the city   **(4)** the problems of the poor

_____ **35.** With which of the following statements would a nativist agree?

(1) "Immigrants must search for opportunity in the United States."

(2) "Immigrants help make this country a better place in which to live."

(3) "Immigrants need to work together to acculturate."

(4) "Immigrants steal jobs from people who were born in this country."

_____ **36.** Which of the following did NOT contribute to the increasing number of newspaper readers in the late 1800s?

(1) desire to learn about current events

(2) newspapers' focus on women's rights issues

(3) compulsory education

(4) growth of the cities

Transforming the Nation

Part II: Constructed-Response Question

DIRECTIONS: *Answer the questions that follow the written and visual documents using the space provided. Base your answers to questions 1, 2, and 3 on the line graph and reading below and on your knowledge of social studies.*

And as it [the automobile] came, it changed the face of America. Villages which had once prospered because they were "on the railroad" languished with economic [weakness]; villages on Route 61 bloomed with garages, filling stations, hot-dog stands, chicken-dinner restaurants, tearooms, tourists' rests, camping sites, and [wealth]. . . . Railroad after railroad gave up its branch lines, or saw its revenues slowly dwindling under the competition of mammoth interurban buses and trucks snorting along six-lane concrete highways. . . . By the end of the decade, what a difference!—red and green lights, blinkers, one-way streets, boulevard stops, [stricter] . . . parking ordinances—and still a shining flow of traffic that backed up for blocks along Main Street every Saturday and Sunday afternoon.
—*Frederick Lewis Allen, 1920s*

Model-T Fords Sold, 1908–1916

1. In which single year were the most Model-T Fords sold? _____

   _____

   _____

2. How did the automobile affect the American landscape? _____

   _____

   _____

3. How did inventions such as the automobile assembly line contribute to economic

   and social changes in the early 1900s? _____

   _____

   _____

Transforming the Nation

Part III: Document-Based Question

Theme: Industrialization

This question is based on the accompanying documents (1–7). This question is designed to test your ability to work with historical documents. Some of the documents have been edited for the purposes of the question. As you analyze the documents, take into account the source of each document and any point of view that may be presented in the document.

Historical Context:
Industrialization, or the process by which the United States changed from a farm to a manufacturing economy, brought about tremendous economic growth as well as growing pains for the nation.

Task:
Using information from the documents and your knowledge of social studies, answer the questions that follow each document in Part A. Your answers to the questions will help you write the Part B essay in which you will be asked:

> • In the late 1800s, the United States economy was changed by the new inventions, remarkably rapid growth, and new forms of transportation and communication. What benefits did these changes bring about? What problems did they cause?

Part A: Short-Answer Questions
Directions: Analyze the documents, and answer the short-answer questions that follow.

Document 1 Photograph showing the completion of the transcontinental railroad (1869)

1. What different kinds of people are shown in the photograph? _____

_____

Transforming the Nation

2. How can you tell that the photograph has been posed for the camera? _____

_____

_____

_____

3. How does the photograph suggest the uniting of East and West? _____

_____

_____

_____

Document 2   Historian Sandy Lydon, describing the lives of Chinese immigrants who worked on California railroads, in *Chinese Gold* (1985)

> Between 1875 and 1880 the Chinese built three separate railroads, laid forty-two miles of track, and drilled 2.6 miles of tunnels to stitch Santa Cruz County together and attach it permanently to the world beyond the Santa Cruz Mountains. The Chinese contributed not only their sweat and their muscle, but their lives. At least fifty Chinese were killed in accidents while building those railroads. . . .
>
> Chinese railroad workers on the Santa Cruz Railroad worked six ten-hour days a week and were paid one dollar a day. Two dollars per week [were] deducted from their pay for food, while expenses such as clothing and recreation chipped away at the remaining four dollars.

4. According to Lydon, how did Chinese immigrants contribute to the growth of the railroads? _____

_____

_____

_____

5. How did their work affect California? _____

_____

_____

_____

6. Is the historian sympathetic to the Chinese workers or not? How can you tell?

_____

_____

_____

Transforming the Nation

Document 3   Photograph showing Thomas Edison in his research laboratory in West Orange, New Jersey (late 1800s)

Library of Congress/Corbis

7. What evidence tells us that the photograph was taken in Edison's **research laboratory?**

_____

_____

_____

8. Was Edison posing for the camera? Explain your answer. _____

_____

_____

_____

9. How does the photograph suggest Edison's inventiveness? _____

_____

_____

_____

Transforming the Nation

● **Document 4** Table based on federal government statistics highlighting major American industries (1890)

Ranking of Major Industries		
Investment	**Total Workers**	**Cost of Labor**
Textiles: $1 billion	Textiles: 824,000	Iron and steel: $285 million
Iron and steel: $998 million	Lumber: 548,000	Textiles: $278 million
Lumber: $844 million	Iron and steel: 532,000	Lumber: $202 million
Food processing: $508 million	Food processing: 249,000	Paper and printing: $118 million

Source: John A. Garraty, *The New Commonwealth* (New York: Harper & Row, 1968), p. 82.

10. What were the major American industries in the late 1800s? Which used agricultural products? _____

_____

_____

11. How many workers were employed in these major industries? Which industry had the most workers? _____

_____

12. Which group of workers was better paid: iron- and steelworkers or textile workers? How can you tell? _____

_____

_____

Document 5 Fictional farm woman, describing her vision of the future life of farmers, in the novel *A Spoil of Office* by Hamlin Garland (1891)

I see a time when the farmer will not need to live in a cabin on a lonely farm. I see the farmers coming together in groups. I see them with time to read, and time to visit with their fellows. I see them enjoying lectures in beautiful halls, erected in every village. I see them gather . . . at evening to sing and dance. I see cities rising near them with schools, and churches, and concert halls and theaters. I see a day when the farmer will no longer be a drudge and his wife a bond slave, but happy men and women who will go singing to their pleasant tasks upon their fruitful farms. . . . In that day the moon will be brighter and the stars more glad, and pleasure and poetry and love of life come back to the man who tills the soil.

13. What does Garland's description tell about the life of farmers? _____

_____

_____

14. From the story, what problems did American farmers face in the late 1800s?

_____

_____

15. Could Hamlin's novel be considered an eyewitness source? Why or why not?

_____

_____

Document 6   Andrew Carnegie, describing the beginnings of the American steel industry, in an essay (1901)

> As late as 1810 there were produced in the whole country only 917 tons of steel. . . . It was not [until] 1864, when the last century was almost two-thirds gone, that the revolution in steel manufacture came to us, and the Iron Age began to give way to the new King Steel, for our first Bessemer steel was made in that notable year, and steel [that earlier had cost] from six to seven cents per pound for ordinary grades has since sold at less than one cent per pound.
>
>   There is one element of cost, however, . . . that has not been [reduced], and that is human labor. [Wages have] risen and the tendency is to higher earnings per man.

16. What does Carnegie mean by 'the Iron Age' and 'King Steel'? _____

_____

_____

17. How did steel production change in the late 1800s? _____

_____

_____

18. Why might Carnegie make the point that wages for steelworkers have risen?

_____

_____

● **Document 7** "Mother" Jones, describing how she organized the wives of coal miners to stop a company effort to use replacement workers (called scabs), from her autobiography (1925)

> I told the men to stay home with the children for a change and let the women attend to the scabs. I organized an army of women housekeepers. . . . The day came and the women came with . . . mops and brooms and pails of water. . . .
>
> Up the mountain side, yelling and hollering, [a woman Jones had chosen] led the women, and when the mules came up with the scabs and the coal, she began beating on the dishpan and hollering and all the army joined in with her. . . . Then the mules began to rebel against scabbing. They bucked and kicked the scab drivers and started off for the barn. The scabs started running down hill, followed by the army of women with their mops and pails and brooms. . . .
>
> [Later] the company put up a notice that all demands were [granted].

19. How did Jones's women's "army" defeat the scabs? _____

_____

_____

_____

● **20.** What role did Mother Jones play in the events she describes? _____

_____

_____

_____

21. How reliable is Jones's account of the events? Explain your answer. _____

_____

_____

_____

Part B: Essay
Directions: Write a well-organized essay that includes an introduction, several paragraphs, and a conclusion. Use evidence from at least four documents in the body of the essay. Support your response with relevant facts, examples, and details. Include additional outside information.

> • In the late 1800s, the United States economy was changed by the new inventions, remarkably rapid growth, and new forms of transportation and communication. What benefits did these changes bring about? What problems did they cause?

Name _____ Class _____ Date _____

A New Role for the Nation

Part I: Multiple-Choice Questions

Identify the number of the choice that best completes the statement or answers the question.

_____ 1. Reformers in the Gilded Age criticized the spoils system because it
  (1) reduced the power of the muckrakers.
  (2) spread corruption.
  (3) reduced the number of government appointments.
  (4) led to the rise of the Progressives.

_____ 2. Which statement summarizes the purpose of the Interstate Commerce Act?
  (1) to prohibit businesses from limiting competition
  (2) to prevent labor unions from blocking free trade
  (3) to regulate civil service jobs
  (4) to ban business practices such as pools and rebates

_____ 3. What is one reason the Progressives turned against President William
    Howard Taft?
  (1) He vetoed a law establishing an eight-hour workday for government
      workers.
  (2) He opposed government investigation of child labor problems.
  (3) He fired a Forest Service official in a dispute over the sale of wilderness lands.
  (4) He did not break up as many trusts as President Theodore Roosevelt had.

_____ 4. Muckrakers fought corruption by
  (1) arousing public opinion.   (3) running for political office.
  (2) taking control of large   (4) forming good-government
      corporations.   leagues.

_____ 5. Which of these groups led the crusade against the sale of alcoholic
    beverages?
  (1) National Association for the Advancement of Colored People
  (2) National Woman Suffrage Association
  (3) Women's Christian Temperance Union
  (4) Society of American Indians

_____ 6. What were two of President Woodrow Wilson's Progressive goals?
  (1) to break up trusts and to encourage competition
  (2) to raise tariffs and to lower interest rates
  (3) to control the money supply and to establish an income tax
  (4) to attract foreign businesses and to investigate unions

_____ 7. Which of the following is NOT an example of new opportunities for women in
    the late 1800s?
  (1) Women formed clubs that promoted reforms.
  (2) Women entered the new profession of social work.
  (3) Women won the right to vote in most states.
  (4) Women became lawyers and doctors.

A New Role for the Nation

_____ 8. Which policy of the Society of American Indians eventually caused it to close down?
(1) It supported the abolishment of reservations.
(2) It pressured Congress to repeal the Dawes Act.
(3) It promoted selling reservation land to speculators.
(4) It educated white Americans about Indian life.

_____ 9. Mexican Americans formed self-help groups known as
(1) los nortes.   (3) barrios.
(2) mutualistas.   (4) Mexicanos.

_____ 10. What was the purpose of the 1907 "Gentlemen's Agreement" between the United States and Japan?
(1) to prevent Japanese wives from joining their husbands in the United States
(2) to promote understanding of Japanese culture
(3) to ensure equal treatment for Japanese American workers
(4) to stop Japanese workers from going to the United States

_____ 11. What was the purpose of the Sherman Antitrust Act?
(1) to prohibit rebates and pools
(2) to forbid the use of strikes by labor unions
(3) to regulate businesses that crossed state lines
(4) to prevent big businesses from limiting competition

_____ 12. Which of the following BEST describes how women won the right to vote?
(1) The women's suffrage movement lobbied Congress.
(2) Seneca Falls delegates persuaded President Wilson to approve suffrage.
(3) Under pressure from a few women, Congress passed the Nineteenth Amendment.
(4) Fifty years of effort by suffragists secured approval of the Nineteenth Amendment.

_____ 13. Which statement describes the experiences of African Americans during the Progressive Era?
(1) President Woodrow Wilson ended segregation of government workers by race.
(2) President Theodore Roosevelt blocked the dishonorable discharge of an African American regiment.
(3) African Americans experienced discrimination throughout the United States.
(4) Jim Crow laws ended segregation in public establishments.

_____ 14. Why did European powers agree to the Open Door policy for China that was suggested by the United States?
(1) They believed that colonial powers should share foreign trade opportunities equally.
(2) They needed allies to defend against the power of the Chinese emperor.
(3) They had already exhausted many of China's trade resources.
(4) They feared the power of the United States.

A New Role for the Nation

_____ **15.** What American action prompted the Japanese emperor to sign the Treaty of Kanagawa?
   (1) an American show of force using steam-powered warships
   (2) a belief that Americans would protect Japanese ports from the Germans
   (3) an offer of financial aid to develop more Japanese ports
   (4) a desire to protect Japanese culture from European influences

_____ **16.** What discovery in the 1890s changed American minds about "Seward's Folly"?
   (1) Prospectors found gold.
   (2) Loggers found rich stands of timber.
   (3) Miners found large deposits of copper.
   (4) Drillers found deposits of petroleum and natural gas.

_____ **17.** Which of the following BEST describes the cause of the explosion aboard the United States battleship *Maine*?
   (1) It was a Cuban rebel bomb.
   (2) It was a secret Spanish attack.
   (3) It remains a mystery to this day.
   (4) It is now known to have been an accident.

_____ **18.** Which of the following BEST summarizes the results of the Spanish-American War?
   (1) The United States granted Cuba, Puerto Rico, and the Philippines limited independence.
   (2) The United States granted Cuba, Puerto Rico, and the Philippines full independence.
   (3) The United States returned control of Cuba, Puerto Rico, and the Philippines to Spain.
   (4) The United States returned the Philippines to Spain, but kept Cuba and Puerto Rico.

_____ **19.** Which of these statements BEST explains how the United States gained land in Samoa?
   (1) The Samoan government asked to become an American territory.
   (2) The United States negotiated a deal with European colonial powers.
   (3) The United States defeated the German fleet in a naval battle.
   (4) The United States signed a treaty with the Samoan government.

_____ **20.** From the perspective of the United States, what was the MOST important effect of Commodore Perry's mission to Japan?
   (1) Japan set out to become a modern industrial nation.
   (2) Japan opened two of its ports to American trade.
   (3) Japan became aware of the power of western industrial nations.
   (4) Japanese rulers saw steam-powered ships for the first time.

_____ **21.** Which of the following was NOT a reason that Theodore Roosevelt intervened in Latin American affairs?
   (1) to promote moral diplomacy
   (2) to protect American interests
   (3) to prevent European interference
   (4) to preserve law and order

Name _____ Class _____ Date _____

A New Role for the Nation

_____ **22.** What happened after the United States sent troops into Mexico in the early 1900s?

(1) American troops helped overthrow the government of Venustiano Carranza.

(2) Strained relations between the two nations led to war in 1916.

(3) Strained relations between the two countries stopped short of all-out war.

(4) "Pancho" Villa used Mexican anger to become president of Mexico.

_____ **23.** What two economic considerations caused European countries to seek possessions in Africa and Asia?

(1) the need for raw materials and a desire to control foreign markets

(2) the need for exotic foods and new medicines

(3) the duty to spread their religion and "civilize" other peoples

(4) the desire to keep sailors and shipbuilders off unemployment rolls

_____ **24.** The Roosevelt Corollary was based on what earlier policy forbidding European colonization in the Americas?

(1) the Monroe Doctrine   (3) the Treaty of Kanagawa

(2) the Open Door Policy   (4) the Foraker Act

_____ **25.** What was one of the tensions in Europe that led to World War I?

(1) Russian people united by poverty overthrew their government.

(2) Many people united by language and culture sought self-government.

(3) A German submarine sank the British passenger ship the *Lusitania*.

(4) The Treaty of Versailles placed difficult demands on Germany.

_____ **26.** With which two countries did Austria-Hungary form the Triple Alliance?

(1) Britain and France   (3) Russia and Italy

(2) Britain and Russia   (4) Italy and Germany

_____ **27.** Which of the following was NOT a characteristic of trench warfare?

(1) heavy artillery bombardments

(2) attacks and counterattacks across open land

(3) short battles with relatively few deaths

(4) use of poison gases on enemy troops

_____ **28.** How did Germany's sinking of the *Lusitania* increase the risk of war with the United States?

(1) The deaths of many American passengers on the British ship outraged President Wilson.

(2) The sinking hurt the United States economy by halting United States trade with Britain.

(3) American ships responded by blockading German ports.

(4) American ships responded by attacking German submarines.

Name _____ Class _____ Date _____

A New Role for the Nation

_____ **29.** Which of the following was a setback for the Allies in 1917?
  (1) the Zimmerman plot
  (2) the Russian Revolution
  (3) the Battle of the Argonne Forest
  (4) the Treaty of Brest-Litovsk

_____ **30.** Why did Germany launch a "peace offensive" in 1918?
  (1) to negotiate a fair peace treaty
  (2) to persuade the United States to remain neutral
  (3) to attempt a final push to win the war
  (4) to encourage the Allies to accept the armistice

_____ **31.** Which of the following nations would have entered World War I if the Zimmerman plot had succeeded?
  (1) Serbia
  (2) Spain
  (3) Switzerland
  (4) Mexico

_____ **32.** Which of the following population changes occurred during World War I?
  (1) Competition for urban housing forced many Americans to move to the country.
  (2) African Americans and Mexican Americans migrated from the South to cities in the North.
  (3) Large numbers of German Americans were sent back to Germany.
  (4) European immigration to the United States greatly increased.

_____ **33.** How did President Wilson hope to end World War I?
  (1) by halting trade with Europe
  (2) by entering the United States into the war
  (3) by declaring peace without victory
  (4) by providing guns and tanks to the Allies

_____ **34.** Woodrow Wilson's Fourteen Points included all the following EXCEPT
  (1) an end to secret agreements.
  (2) a limit on arms.
  (3) the principle of national self-determination.
  (4) the principle of international alliances.

_____ **35.** President Wilson's goal for the League of Nations was
  (1) to protect the independence of all nations.
  (2) to end the right of national self-determination for Central Powers nations.
  (3) to ensure payment of reparations for losses during war.
  (4) to protect each member nation's own individual interests.

A New Role for the Nation

Part II: Constructed-Response Question

DIRECTIONS: *Answer the questions that follow the written documents using the space provided. Base your answers to questions 1, 2, and 3 on the two readings below and on your knowledge of social studies.*

[Abraham] Lincoln said that the safety of this nation was not in its fleets, its armies, [or] its forts, but in the spirit which prizes liberty as the heritage of all men, in all lands, everywhere. . . .

If we have an imperial policy we must have a great standing army as its natural and necessary complement. . . .

A large standing army is . . . the personification of force, and militarism will inevitably change the ideals of the people and turn the thoughts of our young men from the arts of peace to the science of war. . . .

—William Jennings Bryan, 1900

. . . [Shall] we occupy new markets for what our farmers raise, our factories make, our merchants sell . . . ?

. . . The resources and the commerce of these immensely rich dominions will be increased. . . . In Cuba, alone, there are 15,000,000 acres of forest unacquainted with the ax, exhaustless mines of iron, priceless deposits of manganese, millions of dollars' worth of which we must buy, today, from the Black Sea districts. . . .

The riches of the Philippines have hardly been touched by the finger-tips of modern methods. And they produce what we consume, and consume what we produce. . . .

—Senator Albert J. Beveridge, 1898

1. Which writer supports imperialism? Why? _____
   _____
   _____
   _____

2. What reasons does the anti-imperialist give to support his stand? _____
   _____
   _____
   _____

3. What effects did the growth of imperialist feeling have on the United States?
   _____
   _____

A New Role for the Nation

Part III: Document-Based Question

Theme: Global Interaction

This question is based on the accompanying documents (1–8). This question is designed to test your ability to work with historical documents. Some of the documents have been edited for the purposes of the question. As you analyze the documents, take into account the source of each document and any point of view that may be presented in the document.

Historical Context:
The increasing economic power of the United States in the late 1800s and early 1900s changed the way it interacted with other nations around the globe.

Task:
Using information from the documents and your knowledge of social studies, answer the questions that follow each document in Part A. Your answers to the questions will help you write the Part B essay in which you will be asked:

> • As the United States developed into a world economic power, it also became a military and political power. What led Americans to become more involved in world affairs? What were some of the consequences of the nation's new role?

Part A: Short-Answer Questions
Directions: Analyze the documents, and answer the short-answer questions that follow.

Document 1 Chart showing territorial growth of the United States

Date	Territory	Area (sq. mi.)	How Acquired
1803	Louisiana	827,987	Purchase from France
1819	Florida	72,101	Treaty with Spain
1845	Texas	389,166	Independent republic, annexed
1846	Oregon	286,541	Treaty with Great Britain
1848	Mexican Cession	529,189	Conquest from Mexico
1853	Gadsden Purchase	29,670	Purchase from Mexico
1867	Alaska	586,400	Purchase from Russia
1898	Hawaiian Islands	6,407	Independent republic, annexed
1898	Philippine Islands	114,400	Conquest from Spain
1898	Puerto Rico	3,435	Conquest from Spain
1899	Wake Island	3	Occupation
1899	American Samoa	76	Division with Germany and Great Britain
1903	Panama Canal Zone	549	Treaty with Panama
1916	Virgin Islands	133	Purchase from Denmark

Name _____ Class _____ Date _____

A New Role for the Nation

1. What were the three largest areas added to the United States, and how was each gained?

   _____

   _____

   _____

2. In what different ways did the United States expand its territory? _____

   _____

   _____

   _____

3. What do all lands obtained in 1867 and after have in common? _____

   _____

   _____

   _____

Document 2   Senator Henry Cabot Lodge, arguing in favor of building a canal in Central America, in a magazine article (early 1890s)

> In the interests of our [trade] . . . we should build the Nicaragua canal, and for the protection of that canal and for the sake of our commercial [leadership] in the Pacific we should control the Hawaiian islands and maintain our influence in Samoa. . . . When the Nicaraguan canal is built, [taking control of] the island of Cuba . . . will become a necessity. . . . The great nations are rapidly absorbing for their future expansion and their present defense all the vast places of the earth. It is a movement which makes for civilization and the advancement of the race. As one of the great nations of the world the United States must not fall out of the line of march.

4. What three reasons does Lodge give for wanting a canal across Nicaragua in Central America? _____

   _____

   _____

   _____

5. How does Lodge think building a canal will lead to greater territorial expansion?

   _____

   _____

   _____

6. Does this document give mostly facts or mostly opinions? Explain your answer.

   _____

   _____

   _____

A New Role for the Nation

Document 3 Graphs, taken from statistics published by the federal government, showing the growth of American trade from 1880 to 1920

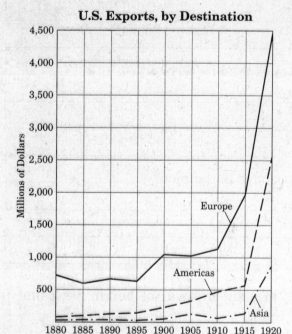

U.S. Exports, by Destination

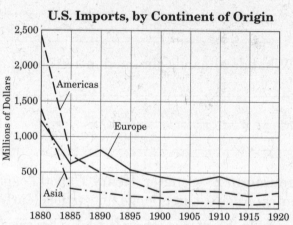

U.S. Imports, by Continent of Origin

7. What was the value of American exports to Europe in 1900? During what period did American exports overall rise dramatically? _____

_____

_____

_____

8. What trend did imports show during the period 1880–1920? _____

_____

_____

_____

9. In 1910, did the United States export more to the Americas than it imported? How can you tell?

_____

_____

_____

A New Role for the Nation

Document 4   Historian Willard Gatewood, describing the attitudes of African Americans toward American expansion in the 1890s, in *Black Americans and the White Man's Burden* (1975)

> In the case of Cuba, [African] Americans [felt] few ideological difficulties; military [action] there promised not only to relieve the island of Spanish rule but also to assure its independence. That many of the islanders were of African descent made it easy for [African Americans] to identify with the cause of [Cuban independence]. . . . Indeed, the role of Afro-Cubans in the struggle for freedom [made believable the] idea that Cuba would become another black republic in the Caribbean . . ..
>
>   [T]he black man's original [doubts] about overseas expansion reemerged in 1899 in . . . opposition to the war in the Philippines. . . . The black community in general [felt a connection] with the Filipinos and tended to take a sympathetic view of [Emilio] Aguinaldo's resistance to American rule.

10. According to Gatewood, why did African Americans support intervention in Cuba?

_____

_____

11. Why did African Americans object to the war in the Philippines? _____

_____

_____

12. Is the author giving a general history of American expansion in the 1800s? Why or why not? _____

_____

_____

Document 5   Campaign ad for Woodrow Wilson's reelection that links opposing candidate Charles Evans Hughes with Theodore Roosevelt, who said the United States should have gone to war over the sinking of the *Lusitania* (1916)

> You Are Working—*Not Fighting!*
> Alive and Happy—*Not Cannon Fodder!*
> Wilson and Peace with Honor?
> or
> Hughes with Roosevelt and War!
>
> The Lesson is Plain:
> If You Want WAR, vote for HUGHES!
> If You Want Peace with Honor
> VOTE FOR WILSON!

A New Role for the Nation

13. How does this campaign ad distinguish between the two candidates?

_____

_____

_____

14. What kinds of words or ideas does the ad attach to Hughes? To Wilson?

_____

_____

_____

15. Does this ad give a balanced view of the two candidates? Why or why not?

_____

_____

_____

Document 6   Woodrow Wilson, requesting a declaration of war on Germany, in a presidential address to Congress (1917)

> Neutrality is no longer [possible] . . . where the peace of the world is involved.
> . . . The menace to that peace and freedom lies in the existence of autocratic
> governments backed by organized force which is controlled wholly by their
> will, not by the will of their people. We have seen the last of neutrality in such
> circumstances. We are at the beginning of an age in which it will be insisted
> that the same standards of conduct and of responsibility for wrong done shall
> be observed among nations and their governments that are observed among
> the [people of those countries].

16. Why does Wilson think that the United States must declare war? _____

_____

_____

_____

17. How does Wilson hope to change the behavior of nations? _____

_____

_____

_____

18. How does this document help explain United States entry into World War I?

_____

_____

_____

A New Role for the Nation

Document 7 Photo showing women streetcar conductors in New York City, hired during World War I (1917–1918)

Courtesy National Archives. photo # (165-WWW-595-E-13)

19. Does the photo express a positive attitude toward the women conductors? Why or why not? _____

_____

_____

_____

20. Why might this photograph have been taken? _____

_____

_____

_____

21. What are two conclusions you could draw from this photo? _____

_____

_____

_____

A New Role for the Nation

Document 8   Political cartoon opposing the League of Nations (1919)

22. Whom do the standing witches represent? How can you tell?

_____

_____

_____

_____

_____

Culver Pictures Inc.

23. What are the standing witches doing to the smaller witches?

_____

_____

_____

_____

24. How can you tell that the cartoonist takes a negative view of the League of Nations?

_____

_____

_____

Part B: Essay

Directions: Write a well-organized essay that includes an introduction, several paragraphs, and a conclusion. Use evidence from at least four documents in the body of the essay. Support your response with relevant facts, examples, and details. Include additional outside information.

> • As the United States developed into a world economic power, it also became a military and political power. What led Americans to become more involved in world affairs? What were some of the consequences of the nation's new role?

Prosperity, Depression, and War

Part I: Multiple-Choice Questions

Identify the number of the choice that best completes the statement or answers the question.

_____ 1. Which of the following statements about officials in the Harding administration is FALSE?

(1) Andrew Mellon balanced the budget and cut taxes.

(2) Herbert Hoover secretly sold food intended for the starving.

(3) Charles Forbes stole millions of dollars from the Veterans Bureau.

(4) Albert Fall took bribes from two oil executives.

_____ 2. The Eighteenth Amendment, sometimes called the "noble experiment," did which of the following?

(1) restricted speculation in the stock market

(2) banned the manufacture, sale, or transportation of liquor

(3) banned anarchists from immigrating to the United States

(4) established company unions to reduce the power of the labor movement

_____ 3. Which of the following BEST summarizes trends in American literature and music in the 1920s?

(1) Talented young people relied on traditional ideas for inspiration.

(2) Talented young people explored original themes and forms.

(3) Literary and musical works created during the decade had little real merit.

(4) Talented young people imitated themes and forms developed in Europe.

_____ 4. How were antiunion feelings related to the "Red Scare"?

(1) Many Americans feared that labor strikes signaled the start of a communist revolution.

(2) Most labor organizations had been heavily infiltrated by anarchists.

(3) Labor leaders called for the overthrow of the government because it failed to support labor.

(4) Most workers were foreigners who favored attacks on well-known Americans.

_____ 5. What group benefited from the passage of the Nineteenth Amendment in 1920?

(1) temperance supporters   (3) labor union organizers

(2) women   (4) law enforcement officers

_____ 6. The issue involved in the Scopes trial was

(1) whether two foreign-born radicals were guilty of murder.

(2) whether police officers had the right to go on strike.

(3) whether the theory of evolution could be taught in public schools.

(4) whether management could force workers to join company unions.

_____ 7. What name was given to the period of achievements of black artists, writers, and musicians in New York during the 1920s?

(1) the Harlem Renaissance   (3) the Roaring Twenties

(2) the Jazz Age   (4) the Red Scare

Prosperity, Depression, and War

_____ **8.** What did Nativists and the Ku Klux Klan have in common during the 1920s?
  (1) The focus of both groups was hatred of African Americans.
  (2) Immigrants were targets for both groups.
  (3) Both groups welcomed the cultural changes taking place.
  (4) Both groups strongly supported the temperance movement.

_____ **9.** Which of the following statements BEST summarizes the relationship between the United States and Latin America during the 1920s?
  (1) The United States returned to its pre–World War I isolationism.
  (2) The United States intervened in Latin America to protect U.S. economic interests.
  (3) The United States sent troops to Mexico to protect oil and mining interests.
  (4) The United States showed its disapproval of the Nicaraguan government by encouraging a revolution in that country.

_____ **10.** Which statement BEST summarizes the results of the 1928 presidential election?
  (1) Republican Herbert Hoover carried the big cities; Democrat Al Smith won in rural areas.
  (2) Voters in big cities were split evenly between the Democratic and Republican candidates.
  (3) Voters in rural areas were split evenly between the Democratic and Republican candidates.
  (4) Republican Herbert Hoover carried rural areas; Democrat Al Smith won in the big cities.

_____ **11.** Which of the following statements does NOT describe one of the ways women's lives changed in the 1920s?
  (1) They gained the right to vote.
  (2) They won the protections of an equal rights amendment.
  (3) They found new employment opportunities.
  (4) Their housework was made easier by electric appliances.

_____ **12.** Which of the following was NOT a way in which Americans were affected by the Great Depression?
  (1) Farmers were unable to grow food.
  (2) Pressures caused some families to split up.
  (3) Many people lost their homes.
  (4) One in four workers lost their jobs.

_____ **13.** Which of the following BEST explains why most Americans voted for Franklin Roosevelt in 1932?
  (1) Franklin Roosevelt inspired them with his confidence.
  (2) Franklin Roosevelt vowed to continue Hoover's policies.
  (3) Voters feared Hoover's bold ideas.
  (4) Voters believed in Roosevelt's cautious approach.

Prosperity, Depression, and War

_____ **14.** Which of the following summarizes the IMMEDIATE cause of the stock market crash of 1929?

    (1) Investors continued buying stocks on margin.

    (2) Investors who were unable to repay loans tried to sell stocks.

    (3) Brokers asked investors to repay loans.

    (4) Speculators bought stocks at greatly reduced prices.

_____ **15.** Why did the government fail to notice the slowing economy in the mid-1920s?

    (1) President Hoover refused to acknowledge the slowdown.

    (2) The economy was slowing in only a few industries.

    (3) The government had no system to track economic statistics.

    (4) The economy had only just begun to slow down.

_____ **16.** Which of the following was enacted to protect people's savings?

    (1) Wagner Act

    (2) Federal Deposit Insurance Corporation

    (3) National Industrial Recovery Act

    (4) Truth-in-Securities Act

_____ **17.** Which of the following was an effect of the other three?

    (1) high winds   **(3)** overgrazed pasture

    (2) Dust Bowl   **(4)** drought

_____ **18.** How did the Supreme Court initially react to New Deal programs in the 1930s?

    (1) The Court ruled that all New Deal programs were constitutional.

    (2) The Court ruled that New Deal programs did not do enough to solve the crisis.

    (3) The Court refused to hear any cases involving New Deal programs.

    (4) The Court ruled that many New Deal programs were unconstitutional.

_____ **19.** In which of the following pairs was the first event the cause of the second?

    (1) Great Depression begins; stock market crashes

    (2) jobless veterans march to Washington; troops disband Bonus Army

    (3) FDR launches Hundred Days; Brain Trust is formed

    (4) Federal Deposit Insurance Corporation is formed; FDR declares "bank holiday"

_____ **20.** Which generalization can be made about African Americans during the 1930s?

    (1) They made great advances in their struggle for equal rights.

    (2) They made slow progress in their struggle for equal rights.

    (3) They had no support in the White House.

    (4) The New Deal gave them little relief.

_____ **21.** Which of the following could be used to describe BOTH Hitler and Mussolini?

    (1) known as *Il Duce*

    (2) built up military in defiance of the Versailles Treaty

    (3) used economic unrest as a tool

    (4) promised new Roman empire

Prosperity, Depression, and War

_____ **22.** Which statement BEST describes life in the Soviet Union under totalitarian leader Joseph Stalin?

(1) Peasants owned land that they could farm.

(2) Critics of the government were murdered or imprisoned.

(3) Voters could choose between candidates from two political parties.

(4) The government set up a court system based on truth and justice.

_____ **23.** What policy did the United States adopt at the beginning of World War II?

(1) aggression   **(3)** appeasement

(2) Fascism   **(4)** isolationism

_____ **24.** How did employment conditions change for African Americans during World War II?

(1) Employers with government contracts could not discriminate when hiring.

(2) All employers were forbidden to discriminate when hiring.

(3) Employment of skilled African American workers declined.

(4) Only employers with government contracts could discriminate when hiring.

_____ **25.** What prompted FDR to call December 7, 1941, "a day which will live in infamy"?

(1) the German attack on the Soviet Union

(2) the invasion of Poland by Germany

(3) the Japanese attack on Pearl Harbor, Hawaii

(4) the German bombing of London, England

_____ **26.** What was the IMMEDIATE result of the sneak attack on Pearl Harbor, Hawaii?

(1) The United States declared war on Germany.

(2) The United States stopped selling oil to Japan.

(3) The United States declared war on Japan.

(4) The United States ceded its Pacific territories to Japan.

_____ **27.** What was the purpose of the U.S. government's bracero program?

(1) It instituted curfew programs for German Americans.

(2) It forced Japanese Americans to sell their homes and businesses.

(3) It permitted recruitment of Mexican workers for jobs in the United States.

(4) It provided compensation to Japanese Americans for wartime property losses.

_____ **28.** How did the D-Day invasion of France affect the war in Europe?

(1) It forced the Germans to keep large numbers of troops in the Soviet Union.

(2) It allowed the Allies to carry out their planned invasion of Italy.

(3) It forced the Germans to split their armies between two different fronts.

(4) It forced the Allies to abandon their bases in North Africa.

Prosperity, Depression, and War

_____ **29.** What was the Potsdam Declaration?

    (1) the Allied declaration of war against Germany

    (2) a German ultimatum to the Allies

    (3) a warning to Japan from Allied leaders

    (4) a statement from the Allies condemning the Holocaust

_____ **30.** Which of the following BEST describes the final days of the war in Europe?

    (1) American troops entered Germany from the east.

    (2) American and Soviet troops entered Germany from different directions.

    (3) German troops marched toward the Soviet Union.

    (4) Germany surrendered in order to avoid an invasion by combined Allied forces.

_____ **31.** Which of the following forced Japan to surrender to the Allies in World War II?

    (1) The United States dropped two atomic bombs on Japanese cities.

    (2) The United States captured the island of Okinawa.

    (3) American ground forces invaded Japan's home islands.

    (4) American warships blockaded Japan's major ports.

_____ **32.** Which of the following lists military campaigns of World War II in their correct sequence?

    (1) North Africa, Italy, France, Germany

    (2) Italy, North Africa, France, Germany

    (3) North Africa, France, Italy, Germany

    (4) France, Italy, North Africa, Germany

_____ **33.** To what atrocity does the term *Holocaust* refer?

    (1) the brutal treatment of American and Filipino prisoners on Bataan

    (2) the execution of Nazi and Japanese leaders after World War II

    (3) the aerial bombardment of houses, farms, and factories

    (4) the slaughter of Europe's Jews by the Nazis

_____ **34.** In the United States, people from which of the following groups were sent to "relocation camps" solely because of their ethnic background?

    (1) Mexican Americans   **(3)** Japanese Americans

    (2) African Americans   **(4)** Chinese Americans

_____ **35.** What was the purpose of the Nuremberg trials?

    (1) to make Germany pay reparations for Allied property losses

    (2) to prosecute Nazi leaders for atrocities and war crimes

    (3) to make Germany give back the land it had occupied during the war

    (4) to prosecute those responsible for the relocation of Japanese Americans

Name _____ Class _____ Date _____

Prosperity, Depression, and War

Part II: Constructed-Response Question

DIRECTIONS: *Answer the questions that follow the visual document using the space provided. Base your answers to questions 1, 2, and 3 on the pie chart below and on your knowledge of social studies.*

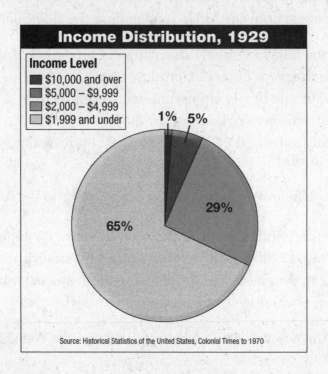

Income Distribution, 1929

Income Level
- ■ $10,000 and over
- ■ $5,000 – $9,999
- ■ $2,000 – $4,999
- □ $1,999 and under

1% 5%

29%

65%

Source: Historical Statistics of the United States, Colonial Times to 1970

1. According to the chart, what percentage of the U.S. population had the greatest income in 1929? _____

   _____

   _____

2. What does the graph demonstrate about the way income was distributed among all Americans at that time? _____

   _____

   _____

3. How does the graph suggest that the United States would soon face an economic crisis? _____

   _____

   _____

Prosperity, Depression, and War

Part III: Document-Based Question

Theme: Changing Role of Government

This question is based on the accompanying documents (1–8). This question is designed to test your ability to work with historical documents. Some of the documents have been edited for the purposes of the question. As you analyze the documents, take into account the source of each document and any point of view that may be presented in the document.

Historical Context:
The American government's role became more active during the middle 1900s so that it could resolve several major problems that arose during that time.

Task:
Using information from the documents and your knowledge of social studies, answer the questions that follow each document in Part A. Your answers to the questions will help you write the Part B essay in which you will be asked:

> • In the 1930s and 1940s, several major problems confronted the American people. To meet these crises, the federal government became more active. What were these crises? How did the government respond to them? How effective were those responses?

Part A: Short-Answer Questions
Directions: Analyze the documents, and answer the short-answer questions that follow.

Document 1   Graph showing changes in the percentage of jobless workers during the 1930s, based on government statistics

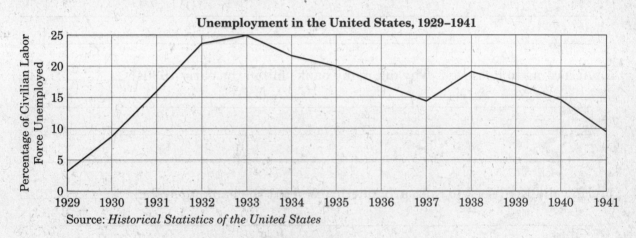

Unemployment in the United States, 1929–1941

Source: *Historical Statistics of the United States*

1. In which years during the 1930s were 15 percent or more of American workers without

   a job? _____

   _____

   _____

Prosperity, Depression, and War

2. About what percentage of Americans were unemployed in 1929? 1933? 1941?

_____

_____

_____

3. What are three facts supported by information on this graph? _____

_____

_____

_____

Document 2 President Franklin D. Roosevelt, trying to persuade Americans to redeposit their money in banks even though many banks recently went out of business, in a radio "fireside chat" (1933)

> My friends . . . when you deposit money in a bank, the bank does not put the money into a safe deposit vault. It invests your money, puts it to work . . . [Why did banks go out of business?] There was a general rush so great that the soundest banks could not get enough currency to meet the demand. . . . [Then he described the plan to gradually reopen banks.] There is no occasion for worry. . . . When people find they can get their money, the phantom of fear will soon be laid [to rest]. I can assure you that it is safer to keep your money in a reopened bank than under the mattress.

4. What do banks do with the money people deposit in them? _____

_____

_____

_____

5. According to Roosevelt, why did many banks fail in the early 1930s? _____

_____

_____

_____

6. How did FDR seek to reassure Americans about the banking system? _____

_____

_____

_____

Document 3 Poor woman, writing to ask for help, in a letter to First Lady Eleanor Roosevelt (1935)

> About a month ago I wrote you asking if you would buy some baby clothes for me with the understanding that I was to repay you as soon as my husband got enough

Prosperity, Depression, and War

work. Several weeks later I received a reply to apply to a Welfare Association so I might receive the aid I need. . . .

   Please Mrs. Roosevelt, I do not want charity, only a chance. . . . As a proof that I am really sincere, I am sending you two of my dearest possessions to keep as [a promise I will repay the loan], a ring my husband gave me before we were married, and a ring my mother used to wear. Perhaps the actual value of them is not high, but they are worth a lot to me.

7. Why is this woman writing to Eleanor Roosevelt? _____

_____

_____

_____

8. How did the woman writing the letter feel about accepting financial help from the

government? _____

_____

_____

9. How does this letter suggest the desperate situation of many Americans in the 1930s?

_____

_____

_____

Document 4   Historian Ronald Takaki, describing steps taken to "repatriate" Mexican Americans, or send them to Mexico, during the Depression, in *A Different Mirror* (1993)

   Blamed for white unemployment, Mexicans became the targets of repatriation programs. . . . Hungry Mexicans were sometimes granted temporary relief by welfare agencies only if they promised to return to Mexico at public expense. . . .

   Repatriation was an employment program for whites—a way to remove a surplus Mexican laboring population and preserve the few remaining jobs for white workers. . . . Altogether, about 400,000 Mexican workers were "repatriated."

10. Why did the government send Mexican Americans to Mexico during the Depression?

_____

_____

_____

11. What does Takaki's description suggest about the impact of economic hard times on

minorities in the United States? _____

_____

_____

Prosperity, Depression, and War

12. Does this document present mostly facts or opinions? Explain your answer.

_____

_____

Document 5 President Roosevelt, banning discrimination against African Americans in the defense industry and the government, in an executive order (1941)

> There shall be no discrimination in the employment of workers in defense industries or government because of race, creed, color, or national origin. . . . It is the duty of employers and of labor organizations . . . to provide for the full and [equal] participation of all workers in defense industries, without discrimination because of race, creed, color, or national origin.

13. What two major employers does Roosevelt's order affect? _____

_____

_____

_____

14. How might this order have affected opportunities for African Americans?

_____

_____

_____

15. Does this document show that discrimination in the United States had ended by

1941? Explain your answer. _____

_____

_____

Document 6 Photograph showing women at work in an airplane factory during World War II (1940s)

UPI/Corbis-Bettmann

Prosperity, Depression, and War

16. What does this photograph show about the kind of work women did during World

War II? _____

_____

_____

17. What message did the photograph send to Americans? _____

_____

_____

18. What is one conclusion supported by evidence in this photograph? _____

_____

_____

Document 7 Photograph showing Japanese Americans who were being taken from their homes and sent to a "relocation camp" (1940s)

Courtesy National Archives

19. Is this photograph an eyewitness account of what happened to Japanese Americans during World War II? Why or why not?

_____

_____

20. What is one statement of fact you can make based on the evidence in this photograph?

_____

_____

Prosperity, Depression, and War

Document 8 President Truman, informing Americans that the first atomic bomb had been dropped on Japan, in a radio address (1945)

> We have spent $2,000,000,000 on the greatest scientific gamble in history and won.
>
> But the greatest marvel is not the size of the enterprise, its secrecy or its cost, but the achievement of scientific brains in putting together . . . complex pieces of knowledge held by many men in different fields of science into a [plan that could work]. And hardly less marvelous has been the [ability] of industry to design, and of [workers] to [run], the machines . . . to do things never done before so that the brain child of many minds came forth in physical shape as it was supposed to do. Both science and industry worked under the direction of the United States Army, which [won] a [great] success in managing so [difficult] a problem.

21. How does Truman show his pride in American achievements? _____

_____

_____

_____

22. Which groups worked together to produce the atomic bomb? _____

_____

_____

_____

23. How did the atomic bomb project reflect the strong hand of government? _____

_____

_____

_____

Part B: Essay

Directions: Write a well-organized essay that includes an introduction, several paragraphs, and a conclusion. Use evidence from at least four documents in the body of the essay. Support your response with relevant facts, examples, and details. Include additional outside information.

> • In the 1930s and 1940s, several major problems confronted the American people. To meet these crises, the federal government became more active. What were these crises? How did the government respond to them? How effective were those responses?

The Bold Experiment Continues

Part I: Multiple-Choice Questions

Identify the number of the choice that best completes the statement or answers the question.

_____ **1.** Which of these events did NOT take place in 1949?
  (1) Fifty-one nations ratified the United Nations charter.
  (2) The Soviet Union tested an atomic bomb.
  (3) Communists seized power in China.
  (4) China's Nationalist government retreated to Taiwan.

_____ **2.** Which of the following is an example of the Marshall Plan at work?
  (1) The Soviet Union blockaded the city of Berlin.
  (2) The United Nations sent military forces to Korea.
  (3) The Untied States helped France rebuild its economy.
  (4) The United States set up the North Atlantic Treaty Organization.

_____ **3.** Which of the following phrases best defines the term *Cold War?*
  (1) conflict between armed opponents
  (2) competition for economic and political power
  (3) conflict that involves exchange of atomic weapons
  (4) competition for petroleum resources in the Arctic

_____ **4.** Who were the two main adversaries in the Cold War?
  (1) Germany and the Soviet Union
  (2) the United States and the Soviet Union
  (3) East Germany and West Germany
  (4) the United States and China

_____ **5.** Which of the following increased worker productivity in the 1950s?
  (1) baby boom   **(3)** new technology
  (2) forty-hour workweek   **(4)** suburban development

_____ **6.** How did discrimination affect the lives of African Americans and Latinos in the United States after World War II?
  (1) They were barred from most public facilities.
  (2) They were not allowed to attend public schools.
  (3) Adults were prevented from learning adequate job skills.
  (4) Children were prevented from attending schools with white children.

_____ **7.** Which of the following declared that "separate-but-equal" public schools were unconstitutional?
  (1) *Hernández* v. *Texas*   **(3)** *Brown* v. *Board of Education*
  (2) *Plessy* v. *Ferguson*   **(4)** Civil Rights Act

The Bold Experiment Continues

_____ 8. Which of the following down NOT describe an American lifestyle change in the 1950s?
(1) Many people moved to new housing developments in the suburbs.
(2) Jobs in the defense and oil industries brought a population boom to the Southwest.
(3) A new public transportation network made Americans less dependent on automobiles.
(4) Rock-and-roll became the favorite musical form of many younger people.

_____ 9. What action led the Senate to censure Senator Joseph McCarthy?
(1) McCarthy condemned Alger Hiss for passing secrets to the Soviet Union.
(2) McCarthy opposed the Communist party.
(3) McCarthy accused Julius and Ethel Rosenberg of spying for the Soviet Union.
(4) McCarthy insisted that there were Communists in the United States Army.

_____ 10. How did the United States respond to the Soviet Union's Berlin blockade?
(1) airlifted supplies to the people of Berlin
(2) withdrew its troops from Germany
(3) sent troops into the Soviet zone of Germany
(4) built a wall between East Berlin and West Berlin

_____ 11. Which of the following was a result of the Cuban Missile Crisis?
(1) Cuban exiles attempted to invade Cuba.
(2) The United States and the Soviet Union reached a compromise about Cuba.
(3) The government of Cuba no longer accepted Soviet aid.
(4) The Soviet Union completed its missile bases in Cuba.

_____ 12. What impact did the Tet Offensive in January 1968 have on the war in Vietnam?
(1) Viet Cong military victories persuaded the United States to withdraw from South Vietnam.
(2) American and South Vietnamese military victories forced the Viet Cong to surrender.
(3) Support for the war increased in the United States.
(4) Opposition to the war increased in the United States.

_____ 13. Which of the following was NOT part of the impact of the Vietnam War?
(1) Nearly 60,000 Americans soldiers died.
(2) Large numbers of Vietnamese refugees fled to the United States.
(3) Differing opinions about the war divided the American people.
(4) A noncommunist government was installed in a reunited Vietnam.

_____ 14. Which of the following MOST directly led to the increase in protest movements in the 1960s?
(1) the GI Bill of Rights
(2) the counterculture movement
(3) the increase in the number of Asian immigrants
(4) the desegregation of public schools

Name _____ Class _____ Date _____

The Bold Experiment Continues

_____ **15.** How did changes to immigration laws in 1965 affect new immigrants?
  (1) The changes made it easier for non-European immigrants to enter the country.
  (2) The changes made it more difficult for Latin American immigrants to enter the country.
  (3) The changes eased penalties for employers who hired illegal immigrants.
  (4) The changes banned illegal immigrants from receiving health care services.

_____ **16.** Which of the following BEST describes the result of the Watergate affair?
  (1) President Nixon was impeached and removed from office.
  (2) President Nixon fired his Vice President, Spiro Agnew.
  (3) President Nixon resigned from office.
  (4) President Nixon was impeached but acquitted by the Senate.

_____ **17.** What was a leading principle of the Carter administration?
  (1) build the Great Society
  (2) help the silent majority
  (3) return power to the states
  (4) defend human rights around the world

_____ **18.** The Voting Rights Act of 1975 was the result of the efforts of which group?
  (1) Latinos   **(3)** African Americans
  (2) Asian Americans   **(4)** The women's rights movement

_____ **19.** In which of the following pairs was the first event or development a direct cause of the second?
  (1) passage of the Federal-Aid Highway Act; dramatic growth in the Sunbelt
  (2) American involvement in Vietnam; the antiwar movement
  (3) Ruling in *Brown* v. *Board of Education of Topeka*; Montgomery bus boycott
  (4) The Watergate affair; Vice President Spiro Agnew is forced to resign

_____ **20.** Which of these people became a leader of the women's rights movement in the 1960s?
  (1) Phyllis Schlafly   **(3)** Rosa Parks
  (2) Betty Friedan   **(4)** Anne Moody

_____ **21.** What was the MOST severe economic problem that President Nixon faced?
  (1) slow economic growth   **(3)** stagflation
  (2) high unemployment   **(4)** inflation

The Bold Experiment Continues

_____ **22.** Which of these groups would MOST likely be affected by bilingual education laws?

  (1) Latinos and African Americans

  (2) African Americans and Asian Americans

  (3) Latinos and Asian Americans

  (4) women and veterans

_____ **23.** Which of the following contributed the MOST to the fall of the Soviet Union?

  (1) President Nixon's policy of détente

  (2) the collapse of a flawed economic system

  (3) the United States boycott of the 1980 Olympics

  (4) the destruction of the Berlin Wall

_____ **24.** What was a frequent result of the growth of political freedom in various countries around the world in the 1980s and 1990s?

  (1) buildup of nuclear arsenals **(3)** economic freedom

  (2) rule by the military **(4)** sanctions

_____ **25.** How did passing the Americans With Disabilities Act help people with physical and mental impairments?

  (1) It guaranteed them public education.

  (2) It protected them against job discrimination.

  (3) It guaranteed them health care.

  (4) It guaranteed them the right to vote.

_____ **26.** All the following were examples of President Reagan's conservative goals EXCEPT

  (1) reducing the size of the federal government.

  (2) balancing the federal budget.

  (3) establishing a national system of health insurance.

  (4) emphasizing traditional values.

_____ **27.** Which of the following occurrences during the presidency of George H. W. Bush was an effect of the other three?

  (1) tax increases **(3)** recession

  (2) downsizing **(4)** banking crisis

_____ **28.** Which of the following decided the outcome of the 2000 presidential election?

  (1) The Supreme Court stopped a recount of disputed votes in Florida.

  (2) Al Gore won the popular vote.

  (3) Al Gore conceded the election to George Bush.

  (4) Al Gore asked for a hand recount in several Florida precincts.

The Bold Experiment Continues

_____ **29.** Which list identifies the three regions from which MOST recent immigrants have come?

   (1) Latin America, western Europe, the Caribbean

   (2) Asia, eastern Europe, Latin America

   (3) Latin America, the Caribbean, Asia

   (4) western Europe, Africa, Latin America

_____ **30.** What is the main reason that post–Cold War Presidents have prompted democracy in countries around the world?

   (1) to strengthen the United States

   (2) to eliminate corruption in those countries

   (3) to eliminate human rights abuses in those countries

   (4) to encourage unification in countries that are split apart by warring factions

_____ **31.** The 1995 peace plan known as the Dayton Accord concerned which region of the world?

   (1) Palestine   **(3)** Northern Ireland

   (2) Somalia   **(4)** Bosnia

_____ **32.** Which is the MOST common way large numbers of older Americans have increased their political influence?

   (1) running for public office

   (2) staging public protests

   (3) supporting the Americans with Disabilities Act

   (4) exercising their right to vote

_____ **33.** On which of the following countries did the United States enforce sanctions to end apartheid?

   (1) South Africa   **(3)** Cuba

   (2) China   **(4)** North Korea

_____ **34.** At the end of the Cold War, American Presidents argued that the United States

   (1) no longer had to be concerned with international affairs.

   (2) had a responsibility to use its power wisely.

   (3) was not affected by the economic crisis in Asia.

   (4) should have prevented the collapse of the Soviet Union.

_____ **35.** Which of the following best describes the involvement of the United States in the Israeli-Palestinian conflict?

   (1) sending military aid to the Palestinians

   (2) blocking oil shipments to Arab countries

   (3) persuading Israel and the PLO to negotiate

   (4) calling for Palestinian self-rule

The Bold Experiment Continues

Part II: Constructed-Response Question

DIRECTIONS: *Answer the questions that follow the written and visual documents using the space provided. Base your answers to questions 1, 2, and 3 on the reading and bar chart below and on your knowledge of social studies.*

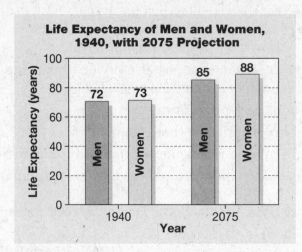

. . . [P]eople are spending a growing proportion of their lives in retirement [and will need] additional years of [Social Security] benefit payments. While longer life spans are clearly desirable, they also mean additional years of benefit payments, and a dramatic long-term increase in Government obligations.

In addition, . . . [as] a result of declining birth rates and increasing life expectancy, the ratio of workers [paying into Social Security] to Social Security beneficiaries is expected to shrink from 5:1 in 1960 to 3:4 today to 2:1 in 2030.

Source: Bush, George W. "Modernize and Reform Social Security." *A Blueprint For New Beginnings.* P. 45. http://www.whitehouse.gov/news/usbudget/blueprint/bud04.html (accessed October 8, 2003).

1. According to the chart, by how many years are the life expectancies of men and women projected to increase between 1940 and 2075? _____

_____

_____

2. Why will lower birth rates make it even harder for the government to pay social security benefits to retired people in the future? _____

_____

_____

3. What are some of the problems that face the elderly in the United States today?

_____

_____

_____

The Bold Experiment Continues

Part III: Document-Based Question

Theme: World Leadership

This question is based on the accompanying documents (1–8). This question is designed to test your ability to work with historical documents. Some of the documents have been edited for the purposes of the question. As you analyze the documents, take into account the source of each document and any point of view that may be presented in the document.

Historical Context:
In the last decades of the 1900s, the United States took on a new international leadership role.

Task:
Using information from the documents and your knowledge of social studies, answer the questions that follow each document in Part A. Your answers to the questions will help you write the Part B essay in which you will be asked:

> • The era after the Allied victory in World War II has been called the American peace. Unlike the other nations that fought, the United States emerged from the war undamaged. It was a great industrial power, a military superpower, and a land of widespread prosperity. In what ways did the United States play a leadership role in the closing decades of the twentieth century? What problems were associated with that role?

Part A: Short-Answer Questions
Directions: Analyze the documents, and answer the short-answer questions that follow.

Document 1   President Harry Truman, announcing the Truman Doctrine to try to prevent the spread of communism in Europe, in a speech (1947)

> It is necessary only to glance at a map to realize that the survival and integrity of the Greek nation are of grave importance in a much wider situation. If Greece should fall under the control of an armed minority, the effect upon its neighbor, Turkey, would be immediate and serious. Confusion and disorder might well spread throughout the entire Middle East. . . .
>
>   The free peoples of the world look to us for support in maintaining their freedoms.

1. What countries and regions does Truman see as threatened by communism?

_____

2. Why does Truman say that the United States must be a world leader?

_____

_____

3. How did Truman see the world situation in 1947? _____

_____

The Bold Experiment Continues

Document 2   Reverend Ake Zetterberg, Swedish minister, commenting on why he thought Martin Luther King, Jr., deserved the Nobel Peace Prize, in a speech (1964)

> Martin Luther King, in our view, has long deserved the Peace Prize. He is a personality dedicated to nonviolence. . . . He has proved that he can take setbacks without losing courage or abandoning his ideals. His unarmed struggle is a model case, a pattern to inspire colored people all over the world.

4. Why did Martin Luther King, Jr., receive the Nobel Peace Prize? _____

_____

_____

5. According to Zetterberg, what strengths did King exhibit? _____

_____

_____

6. How did Zetterberg believe King offered an example to the world? _____

_____

_____

Document 3   Roy Hoopes writing about his experience as a Peace Corps volunteer in the 1960s

> Ideas [cannot be separated] from the manner and place in which they are lived. This to me is the meaning of the Peace Corps as a new frontier. It is the call to go, not where man has never been before, but where he has lived differently; the call to experience firsthand the intricacies of a different culture. . . .
>   . . . My instincts revolt against the whole idea of having to prove in some . . . way the value of the Peace Corps. If the aim is to help people, I understand that in the sense of the Ibo proverb which says that when the right hand washes the left, the right hand becomes clean also.

7. How does Hoopes see the Peace Corps as a "new frontier"? _____

_____

_____

8. According to Hoopes, how did Peace Corps work benefit the volunteers as much as

those they went to help? _____

_____

_____

9. Does this document express mostly facts or opinions? Explain your answer.

_____

_____

The Bold Experiment Continues

Document 4   Photo showing a Vietnam War veteran honoring dead comrades at the Vietnam Veterans Memorial in Washington, D.C. (1982)

UPI/Corbis-Bettmann

10. How does the photograph capture a sense of both the living and the dead?

_____

_____

11. What feelings might the photographer hope to arouse? _____

_____

_____

12. Can you tell the photographer's attitude toward the Vietnam War? Explain your answer.

_____

_____

Document 5   President Jimmy Carter, message placed inside the *Voyager* spacecraft, which was launched to first explore certain planets and then leave the solar system (1977)

> This Voyager spacecraft was constructed by the United States of America. We are a community of 240 million human beings among the more than 4 billion who inhabit the planet Earth. We human beings are still divided into nation states, but these states are rapidly becoming a single global civilization.

13. What audience was Carter addressing in this message? _____

_____

_____

14. Was Carter expressing facts or opinions? Explain your answer. _____

_____

_____

The Bold Experiment Continues

Document 6 President Ronald Reagan, explaining why he placed American soldiers in Lebanon, in a speech (1983)

> Why should our young men be dying in Lebanon? Why is Lebanon important to us?
>   . . . Every President who has [held] this office in recent years has [known] that peace in the Middle East is of vital concern to our nation and . . . Western Europe and Japan. . . . The area is key to the economic and political life of the West. . . .
>   Now there was a time when our national security was based on a standing army . . . here within our own borders and . . . a navy to keep the sea lanes open for shipping things necessary to our well being. The world has changed. Today our national security can be threatened in far-away places.

15. Why does Reagan think the United States must intervene in Lebanon?

_____

_____

16. How did Reagan explain the need for American involvement in foreign countries in general? _____

_____

_____

17. According to Reagan, how was the world different from how it had been?

_____

_____

Document 7 Walter Isaacson, writing about the impact of the computer revolution, in a *Time* magazine article (1998)

> [The] Digital Revolution is now [changing] the end of this century the way the Industrial Revolution [changed] the end of the last one. Today, millions of transistors, each costing far less than a staple, can be [placed] on wafers of silicon. On these microchips, all the world's information and entertainment can be stored . . . , processed and zapped to every [corner of the world].
>   . . . The microchip has become—like the steam engine, electricity and the assembly line—an advance that [starts] a new economy.

18. To Isaacson, how is the Digital Revolution like the Industrial Revolution?

_____

_____

_____

19. How has the Digital Revolution changed people's lives? _____

_____

_____

The Bold Experiment Continues

20. Does Isaacson have a positive or negative view of the Digital Revolution? How can

you tell? _____

_____

_____

Document 8   Theodore White, discussing what it means to be an American, in a newspaper column on the 210th anniversary of the Declaration of Independence (1986)

> Jefferson himself could not have imagined the reach of his call across the world in time to come when he wrote: "We hold these truths to be self-evident, that
> all men are created equal, that they are endowed by their Creator with certain unalienable rights." . . .
>   But over the next two centuries the call would reach the potato patches of Ireland, the ghettoes of Europe, the [rice paddies] of China, stirring farmers to leave their lands and townsmen their trades. . . .
>   What is most important is the story of the idea that made [these people] into a nation, the idea that had an explosive power undreamed of in 1776. . . .
>   Americans are a nation born of an idea; not the place, but the idea, created the United States government.

21. What powerful idea does White say Jefferson launched in 1776? _____

_____

_____

22. How did that idea affect the world? _____

_____

_____

23. What is White's view of the Declaration of Independence? _____

_____

_____

Part B: Essay

Directions: Write a well-organized essay that includes an introduction, several paragraphs, and a conclusion. Use evidence from at least four documents in the body of the essay. Support your response with relevant facts, examples, and details. Include additional outside information.

> • The era after the Allied victory in World War II has been called the American peace. Unlike the other nations that fought, the United States emerged from the war undamaged. It was a great industrial power, a military superpower, and a land of widespread prosperity. In what ways did the United States play a leadership role in the closing decades of the twentieth century? What problems were associated with that role?

Acknowledgments

Grateful acknowledgment is made to the following for copyrighted material:

Page 20 Document 1: From *A Different Mirror: A History of Multicultural America* by Ronald Takaki. Copyright © 1993 by Ronald Takaki. **Page 22** Document 4: From *From Slavery to Freedom: A History of Negro Americans* by John Hope Franklin. Copyright © 1980 by Alfred A. Knopf, Inc. **Pages 22–23** Document 5: From pages 72–73 in *The Cultural Life of the American Colonies* by Louis B. Wright. Copyright © 1957 by Harper & Brothers, renewed 1985 by Frances B. Wright. **Pages 23–24** Document 7: From *A Different Mirror: A History of Multicultural America* by Ronald Takaki. Copyright © 1993 by Ronald Takaki. **Page 24** Document 8: From *Adams Family Correspondence*, Volume I, edited by L. H. Butterfield. Copyright © 1963 by the Massachusetts Historical Society. **Page 35** Document 9: From *American Mosaic: The Immigrant Experience in the Words of Those Who Lived It* by Joan Morrison and Charlotte Fox Zabusky. Copyright © 1980 by Joan Morrison and Charlotte Fox Zabusky. **Page 43** Document 3: Excerpts from *The Journals of Lewis and Clark* edited by Bernard DeVoto. Copyright © 1953 by Bernard D Voto. Renewed 1981 by Avis DeVoto. **Pages 54–55** Document 2: From "Petition by Cherokee Women, 1818" from The Archives of the American Board of Commissioners for Foreign Missions. **Page 56** Document 5: From *A Different Mirror: A History of Multicultural America* by Ronald Takaki. Copyright © 1993 by Ronald Takaki. **Page 93** Document 4: From *Black Americans and the White Man's Burden, 1898–1903* by Willard B. Gatewood, Jr. Copyright © 1975 by Willard B. Gatewood, Jr. **Pages 104–105** Document 3: From *Down and Out in the Great Depression: Letters of the Forgotten Man* edited by Robert S. McElvaine. Copyright © 1983 by the University of North Carolina Press. **Page 105** Document 4: From *A Different Mirror: A History of Multicultural America* by Ronald Takaki. Copyright © 1993 by Ronald Takaki. **Page 116** Document 3: From *The Peace Corps Experience* edited by Roy Hoopes. Copyright © 1968 by Roy Hoopes. **Page 118** Document 7: From "Man of the Year" in *Time*, 12/27/97. Copyright © 1997 by Time, Inc. **Page 119** Document 8: From *The New York Times Magazine*, January 1, 1986. Copyright © 1986 by The New York Times Co.

Note: Every effort has been made to locate the copyright owner of material reprinted in this book. Omissions brought to our attention will be corrected in subsequent editions.